THE OWNER'S COMPREHENSIVE GUIDE TO
TRAINING AND SHOWING
YOUR DOG

MARIE CAHILL

THE OWNER'S COMPREHENSIVE GUIDE TO

TRAINING AND SHOWING

YOUR DOG

MARIE CAHILL

MALLARD
PRESS

Acknowledgements

The author would like to express her grati-
tude to the American Kennel Club, the Australian National Kennel Council, the Canadian
Kennel Club, the Irish Kennel Club, the Kennel
Club of England, the New Zealand Kennel
Club, and the United Kennel Club, particularly
Andy Johnson, for their assistance. She would
also like to thank Sarah and Amanda for
explaining how dogs think.

Page 1: **A woman and her Afghan Hound
spend a few final minutes rehearsing for
an All Breed Show.** *Page 2-3:* **A trio of
adorable Pug puppies.** *Page 4, from top
to bottom:* **A game of fetch combines
obedience training with fun; Praise is an
essential element of training; Oakdale's
Sundance Miracle celebrates after winning points in a United Kennel Club
Licensed Hunt.**

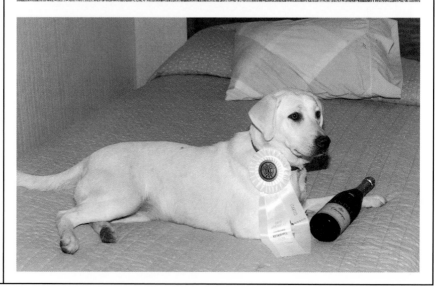

CONTENTS

TRAINING YOUR DOG

Above: **The Chihuahua.** *Facing page:* **The Collie's heritage as a working dog makes the breed a diligent and willing pupil.**

INTRODUCTION

The dog has been man's companion through the ages. This centuries old friendship is due, in part, to the dog's ability to be trained. Dogs are pack animals and will instinctively follow the orders of the leader of the pack–the owner.

Dogs are intelligent animals. Scientists and lay people alike debate the issue of the dog's intelligence, for which there is no easy answer. Dogs cannot think like humans do, but they are capable of understanding quite a lot. Simple phrases and words are not beyond a dog's understanding, as many dog owners can testify–'Amanda, eat your crunchies,' or 'Sarah, go to sleep.' How does the dog understand? A dog owner might argue that a dog has the mind of a small child, while others contend that the dog has simply learned the command. Some people measure a dog's intelligence by how quickly he learns; others might point to a dog's ability to sense his owner's mood as a sign of intelligence.

Dogs, like people, learn at different rates, but with a little patience and consistency, all dogs, with few exceptions, should be able to be trained to come when called, to walk calmly beside their masters, and to lie down quietly and obediently. A well-trained dog will not beg from the table; he won't destroy the furniture in your living room or the roses in your garden.

Although dogs can be easily trained, training a dog requires commitment on the owner's part. A dog needs frequent lessons; a training session every other week will not be enough to train a dog. A human being could not learn how to play the piano if he sat down for twenty minutes once a week. Only through repetition, firmness and consistency will your dog learn.

Tone of voice conveys much to your dog. When you want him to come or play fetch, generate some excitement with your voice. When you want him to heel or to stop chewing on your Italian leather shoes, use a firm voice. A conversational tone will get you nowhere. Some people, particularly women, have a difficult time learning to project a powerful tone of voice. For these people, hand signals used in conjunction with voice commands effectively convey a sense of authority to the dog.

Above: **Talking to your dog is an important part of training. A dog can understand when she has done well and will strive to please her owner.**

Dogs want to please. Dogs understand when they have done wrong and can learn from their mistakes. If a dog senses your anger or displeasure, he will take notice—unlike a cat, which understands but usually chooses to ignore you. It is up to the owner to let the dog know that he has done wrong, and the scolding must be clearly associated with the misbehavior. A puppy that has made a mess on the kitchen floor will not understand what he has done wrong if the scolding comes two hours after the fact.

TRAINING YOUR PUPPY

The first—and easiest—lesson your puppy will need to learn is his name. If you always address your puppy by his name, he will soon respond. Avoid using nicknames that might confuse your puppy.

Next teach your puppy the meaning of the word 'NO.' Puppies are curious creatures and will want to explore their new surroundings. Your new puppy is bound to get into trouble sooner or later–he will want to chew on an electric cord or pounce on your cat or bite your toes. The first word your puppy learns, 'No,' will be an invaluable command throughout your dog's life. It will stop him from urinating on your kitchen floor, or from jumping up and ruining your pantyhose. 'No' is often used in conjunction with 'Bad dog,' a command guaranteed to reduce your dog to shame.

Your vocabulary for training your puppy is not complete without 'OK' and 'Good dog.' 'OK' is an essential part of training; it releases your dog from any command, be it sit, stay or down. As your puppy grows up, he'll turn to you for permission in those situations he's not sure about, and your 'OK' gives him the permission he seeks. Your dog thrives on 'Good dog.' Use it liberally.

HOUSEBREAKING YOUR PUPPY

The best way to housebreak your puppy is to use the crate training method (see text), but if your puppy is alone all day, you will need to use paper training *(above)* as a back up method. Keep the puppy confined in a small area and cover the area with newspapers.

Housebreaking lessons should begin as soon as you bring your puppy home. Take him outside to give him a chance to relieve himself–and then praise the puppy when he does. A puppy should have the opportunity to relieve himself every couple of hours and after every meal.

The only way to housebreak your puppy is to keep an eye on him. Keep in mind that a puppy is a baby, and, like his human counterpart, requires almost constant attention. You will be amazed by how often a young puppy needs to urinate. As a rule of thumb, take your puppy outside after every meal, after playtime, first thing in the morning and last thing at night. Watch also for signs of restlessness, circling the room, or sniffing the ground. Once outside, be sure to praise your puppy *lavishly* when he relieves himself.

At first, it will seem that you are rushing outdoors with your puppy every 20 minutes. Have patience! With each passing day, your puppy will gain better control over his system.

A good practice is to always go to the same spot so the puppy associates that particular spot with relieving himself. Using a simple command, while not necessary, reinforces the idea. Of course, you can't watch your dog every single minute of the day. Accidents are bound to happen, and when they do the puppy should be scolded and taken outside to the proper spot. Then praise it lavishly for being in the right place. Positive reinforcement (praise) works far faster than negative reinforcement (punishment).

The biggest obstacle to housebreaking is what to do with the puppy when you cannot watch it every minute of the day.

Many trainers and veterinarians recommend crate training–putting the puppy in a cage, box or carrier when the owner is unable

Above: A chocolate Labrador Retriever puppy. *Below:* A successful training regimen also includes time for play, for puppies as well as adult dogs.

to keep a constant eye on the youngster. After your puppy has played and/or eaten and had the chance to relieve himself, put him in his box for a short time (no more than an hour or so). At first, he will probably yip to be taken out, but he will soon settle down for a nap. Once you let the puppy out of the cage, be sure to take him outside immediately.

Some owners worry that this is a cruel method for housebreaking a puppy. The method is, in fact, modeled after the system used by Mother Nature herself. A pup, whether a Golden Retriever puppy or a wolf in the wild, will not dirty its own area. During the first few weeks of a puppy's life, his mother will keep the area–be it a whelping pen or wolf's den–clean. Eventually, the litter will observe mother running off to a secluded area to relieve herself and the pups will learn by mimicking mom.

Once accustomed to the cage, most puppies adjust to being left alone and will be perfectly content in a cage for a brief period of time. The cage will function as the puppy's 'home,' and, when given the freedom to go in and out of its cage, your puppy will go to its cage when he is ready for a nap.

The disadvantage of crate training is that a puppy cannot be confined to the cage for an entire day while you are at work. At night, however, the cage is fine, as long as you are willing to jump out of bed at 3:00 AM when you hear the puppy whimpering to go outside. Don't expect your puppy to last through the night until he is about three months old.

During the day, paper training provides a back up for those long hours when the puppy cannot be left in his crate. To paper train a puppy, restrict the puppy to an easily cleaned area, such as the kitchen. Whatever you do, do not let an untrained puppy have the run of the house. Cover the area with newspapers. The puppy will probably develop a preference for one spot, so you can gradually

remove the papers from the rest of the room. Reinforce the idea of using the same spot by placing the puppy there whenever you see the telltale signs of a puppy needing to relieve himself (see above).

The advantage of paper training is that a puppy's system needs to be emptied *often* and the newspapers are convenient if the puppy is left alone for several hours at a time. The disadvantage is that the puppy is being taught that it is acceptable to relieve himself in the house, albeit on a newspaper. A puppy that has been paper trained will have to be retrained to relieve himself outdoors. This can be accomplished by gradually moving the papers to the door and eventually outside.

Though the process will undoubtedly be frustrating at times, dogs are smart animals and your puppy will someday soon be housebroken. How quickly depends on both you and the puppy. It's up to you to recognize the warning signs of a puppy about to relieve himself. In addition, establish a routine so that your puppy expects to go outside after meals, before bed, and so on. Dogs learn by repetition, and your puppy will eventually associate going outside with relieving himself. Feeding your puppy on a regular schedule also aids housebreaking because it helps to regulate the puppy's digestive system.

As with any kind of training, consistency is the key to housebreaking a puppy. Scold your puppy when he does wrong. A harsh word and firm tone of voice is all that is necessary. Some people advocate rubbing a puppy's nose in his mess. This sort of sadistic punishment serves no good purpose.

Above: When your dog successfully completes a lesson, praise her with a 'Good Dog!' and a pat on the head. *Left:* Though only puppies, these Samoyeds are trained to pose for a camera. Their portraits will grace the pages of a calendar, or perhaps appear as a poster.

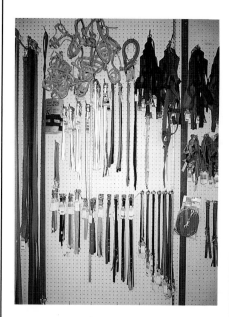

Above: The appropriate leash and collar are essential tools for training your dog. Many professional trainers recommend a leather leash over nylon because the leather provides a better grip, whereas nylon can burn your hand if your dog should pull on the leash suddenly.

EARLY TRAINING

While you are housebreaking your puppy, you should also begin leash training. Some puppies will object to a collar being placed around their necks and will try to remove it, but others won't be fazed by a collar at all. In fact, as your puppy grows up, he will be disturbed if you remove the collar. Make sure the collar is loose enough to slip two fingers underneath it, but not so loose that it will get caught on something.

Getting your puppy used to the leash may prove more difficult, so use the lightest weight leash you can find—a cat leash is perfect. Let your dog wander around the house with the leash on so that he becomes accustomed to it. Dogs love to go for walks and as soon as your puppy associates the leash with a trip outdoors, he won't be bothered by a leash at all.

A very young puppy should not be taken for walks because he runs the risk of infection and will tire easily. However, if you are housebreaking your dog, you obviously need to take your puppy outside. For safety's sake, you should keep the puppy on a leash when you take him outside to relieve himself.

After your puppy has had his shots, you can take him for a walk through the neighborhood and teach him how to walk on a leash. From a young age encourage him to stay close by your side. A firm voice and a gentle tug on the leash should be enough to keep the puppy in line. Serious lessons on how to heel should wait until the puppy is about three and a half months old. If you train your puppy to walk on a leash at a young age, learning to heel will be much easier for him. Do not allow your puppy to chew on the leash while on a walk. The leash is your symbol of authority; it is not a toy.

Part of a puppy's charm is his playful nature, but every owner will need some peace and quiet. A young puppy can be taught to go to his bed or box or the corner of the room and stay there. Use a command like 'Go to sleep,' 'Go lie down' or simply 'Bed.' To teach the command, point to the spot where you want him to stay put. Brightly give the command 'Go to sleep' and run to the designated spot, repeating the command, with a 'Good boy' or two thrown in. If the puppy tries to leave his bed, firmly tell him to 'Stay.' If you are using the crate training method of housebreaking, the crate is an ideal place to put the puppy when you want him to 'Go to sleep.' As in all training, the key is firmness and consistency. If your resolve weakens and you let the puppy out of the box, your puppy will know that he has the upper hand.

An offshoot of this lesson is teaching your puppy to stay by himself. The first time you leave your puppy alone it will bark—a habit which may persist unless the dog is properly trained. To accustom your puppy to being alone, leave him in familiar surroundings. When he barks, make sure he is alright—that he is not asking to go outside, but don't give in and let the puppy get the best of you. Leave the puppy alone!

While they are teething, puppies often chew on things to ease the

pain. To keep your puppy from chewing on your belongings, first make sure he has plenty of toys to chew on. When your puppy does chew on something he should not, reprimand him by firmly telling him 'No' or by giving the command 'Drop it.' Redirect his behavior by giving the puppy one of his toys.

Your puppy will also attempt to chew on you. Again, try to interest him in one of his toys. Pushing the puppy away from you may seem like part of a game to him.

Make sure that the toys you buy for your puppy are safe. The toy should be non-toxic and large enough that it cannot be swallowed; it should be free of sharp edges or pieces that can be chewed off and swallowed. Rawhide chews are especially good for a teething puppy, and almost all dogs enjoy playing with tennis balls. Avoid giving your puppy an old shoe to chew on because a dog cannot differentiate between the shoes that are acceptable to chew on and those that are not.

Above, left to right: **The correct way to put a choke chain on your dog. A choke chain will not hurt your dog. It works by getting the dog's attention with a quick pop-and-release action. Do not allow the dog to strain against the collar. Instead, keep the leash slack and give the collar a quick tug. Make sure the chain pulls from above the dog's neck, not below, so that the chain will release.**

BASIC COMMANDS

Dogs can be trained at any age, but the process will be easier on both of you if you start while the dog is still a puppy, before he has learned any bad habits. When your puppy is three months old, he is old enough to master simple commands. The first commands to teach your puppy are sit, stay, come, heel and down.

Keep training lessons short—about 10 minutes—as a puppy's attention span is not long. The first few lessons should last no longer than five minutes. Train your puppy in an area free of distractions. Reward him with positive reinforcement—'Good dog!'—when he obeys a command rather than scolding him when he does not obey. Lavish praise and a pat on the head or a scratch behind the ears will be much more effective than coaxing him with food. An occasional treat can be used for training, but the dog should learn to obey you without a 'bribe.' Master one lesson before moving on to the next command, and always use the same command. Don't confuse your puppy by alternating 'Come' with 'Come over here right now!'

Above: To teach your dog to sit, hold a small object above his head. He will probably sit in order to see what is in your hand. If he doesn't sit, push his rump down.

Facing page: Notice how closely this Poodle pays attention to his trainer. Your dog should watch *you*–not other dogs or people. Talk to him to keep his attention, but use the choke collar when necessary to keep him in line.

SIT. Use a leash to train your dog to sit. Give the command 'Sit' and push down on the dog's hindquarters with your left hand, while pulling up on the leash with the right. If you pull up and push down at the same time, you will naturally ease your dog into a sitting position. Although dogs learn quickly, your dog will be puzzled at first. He will want to please, but won't know what you want, so keep showing him how to sit. If you start to feel frustrated, you and your dog will both be better off to end the lesson for the time being. If you repeat the lesson every day, your dog will soon understand. Once your dog has obeyed the command to sit several times, take the leash off. He should now obey the command without the reinforcement from the leash. If not, go back to using the leash.

STAY. 'Stay' is a more difficult command because it runs contrary to the dog's desire to be with you. Using the leash again, begin your lesson by running through 'Sit.' With your dog in a sitting position, tell it to 'Stay.' Take up the slack in the leash to keep your dog in place. When the dog starts to move, firmly repeat the command and gradually back away from the dog. Be sure to maintain eye contact

Above: **The sit at heel position. Your dog should automatically sit at heel when you come to a stop.**

with your dog. Reinforce the 'Stay' command by using a hand signal—your hand raised in the air like a police officer directing traffic. As you back away slacken the leash. When the dog appears to understand, try giving the command as you walk around him. Eventually, try the lesson without the leash.

COME. When you call your dog's name, most of the time he will come bounding to your side. At times, however, he will be distracted and won't come running. The command 'Come' teaches your dog to come even when he does not want to.

Begin the lesson by giving your dog the command to stay. Walk away from him and then call him by name, along with the command 'Come.' You may have to give a little tug on the leash to show your dog that you really do want him to come to you. A gesture, such as a clap or slapping your hand against your thigh, will help excite your dog into motion. When your dog does come to you, lavish him with praise—'What a wonderful dog! Sarah, you're such a good girl!' Make your dog want to come to you.

HEEL. Your dog should be taught to heel, both on and off the leash. This lesson will take longer to learn than the other commands and therefore requires more patience on your part. To train your dog to heel you will need a choke collar. A small dog will not need a choke collar, although a nylon choke can be substituted for a metal one. The choke collar should be about two inches longer than the dog's regular collar—it needs to be long enough to pull on and off over the dog's head. To use a choke collar, hold the collar by the rings, one above the other, and drop the chain through the lower ring. Put the collar on so that it pulls from *above* the neck, not below. In this way, the chain will automatically loosen when you let up on the leash. The choke collar will not hurt your dog; it is designed to get your dog's attention by making it feel uncomfortable. Many people have the mistaken idea that a choke is harmful and therefore buy the one with the smallest links because they look less menacing. The reality is that the larger link chain collars are better for the dog.

Use the choke collar *only* for training and walking. If you leave the choke collar on your dog all the time, you run the risk of it getting caught on something. Choke collars also tend to discolor your dog's coat. In addition, you will need a sturdy leash, about six feet long, for training.

Your dog should walk beside you, with his right shoulder next to your left leg. Shorten the leash so that the dog stays near your side and tell him 'Heel' as you start walking. If he starts to pull away, jerk the leash while firmly repeating the command 'Heel!' Continue walking as you jerk the leash. The object is to make your dog walk by your side. Stopping and jerking does not give your dog a clear idea of what you want him to do. As you walk along, speak reassuringly to your dog—he will probably be confused.

When your dog is beginning to understand 'Heel,' teach him how to heel while turning. Right turns are easier to learn, so try them first. If he has trouble heeling while you turn, take a shorter grip on the leash to force him to move with you.

When your dog heels properly with a slack leash, it is time to try heeling without the leash. If your dog doesn't heel as he should without the leash, reprimand him sharply. If that fails, put the leash back on and run through the now familiar routine.

Heeling is more than your dog walking quietly by your side–it is walking by your side even though your dog encounters countless distractions–other dogs, fascinating smells, sticks and stones to pick up and passersby who coo, 'What an adorable dog.' A well-trained dog ignores all distractions, no matter how fascinating. When your dog is doing well with heel, take him for a walk among people. If possible don't stop when people want to pet him, as this will only excite your dog. Keep walking when you see other dogs, and don't stop to let your dog sniff. Teach your dog to sit whenever you stop, whatever the reason–a traffic light, an interesting shop window, a chance encounter with a friend. Eventually, when you take your dog out on a crowded street it will sit politely by your side if and when you decide to stop.

DOWN. Start with your dog in the sit position. You can entice a puppy into the down position by patting the floor in front of him. As you tap the floor, say 'Down.' Some puppies will get down so they can sniff the floor. If your dog does, praise him and pet him so he'll associate good things with lying down. If you dog needs a little extra encouragement, pull his front legs forward and push down on his shoulders as you give the command 'Down.' Alternative methods for putting the dog in the down position are: 1) From a sitting position, lift one front leg while gently pushing the opposite shoulder toward the raised leg. This forces the dog to lie down; or 2) With the leash on, apply pressure on the choke chain with your foot. Release pressure as soon as the dog is down. Repeat this several times until your dog associates the action with the word. Be sure to praise your dog throughout the exercise. When the dog seems comfortable, tell him 'Stay' and back away a foot or so. Gradually increase the time the dog is required to stay down. Do not let the dog up when you see him start to get restless; otherwise the dog will know he has the upper hand in training.

At first you'll think your dog cannot stay in the down position for much longer than a minute. Though it may not seem so at first, a dog can be trained to hold the down position for quite a long time. In an obedience trial, dogs must hold the long down for five minutes while their owners are out of sight. Pet owners can expect no less from their dogs. Your dog can be trained to do a long down for up to an hour. While that may seem like an extraordinarily long time that serves no useful purpose, think again. Keeping the long down reminds the dog who is in charge. A long down for only 15 minutes serves a multitude of purposes. You can use the command to settle your dog down after company arrives, while you are busy with a household task, or while you are waiting for your turn at the vet's office.

Though not necessary when working inside, some dogs work better on the leash, as it adds an air of seriousness to the lesson. Outside, you will definitely need to keep your dog on a leash. Puppies especially will want to run around or just play. When you move your lessons from inside to outside, you may have to start the

Above: **Like this German Shepherd, all dogs can be trained to sit quietly in the heel position when the owner comes to a halt.**

Above: 'Stand' is an essential command for both conformation shows and obedience trials, but the command is also useful for pet owners who need their dogs to hold still for a moment.

lessons from scratch because your dog will be more distracted outdoors. However, your dog will relearn the lessons in no time.

OBEDIENCE SCHOOL

Some owners find it helpful to enroll their dogs in obedience school. Although such classes may conjure up the image of a roomful of bad dogs, obedience schools are really more for the owner than the dog. Training a dog requires a certain amount of knowledge and discipline, and many first time dog owners don't know what to do when confronted with a rambunctious four-month-old puppy. The classes are taught by experienced dog handlers who will guide you and your dog through the intricacies of training. Once shown what to do, anyone–man, woman, or child–can train a dog.

An obedience class will make you practice the lessons–or it should. After all, you are there because you want your dog to learn. A class also gives your dog the chance to interact with other dogs. Why do you want a dog that has social skills with other dogs? Because daily you will encounter other dogs. If your dog is a male, his natural inclination is to growl at other dogs as you pass them on your walk. On the other hand, you may have an overly friendly female who wants to jump all over every dog she meets. Enrolling your dog in a class will help him learn how to control himself when he meets other dogs.

To find a reputable dog school, check with your veterinarian or local humane society. Friends with dogs of their own who have successfully completed a class are another good source. Don't hesitate to check out the school before you enroll your dog. Ideally, the class should be limited to 10 students. Talk with the trainer and/or watch a class. The dogs should be handled firmly, but not beaten into submission.

ADVANCED TRAINING

STAND. 'Stand' is one of the basic commands that the American Kennel Club (AKC) requires for the Companion Dog title. Formally called Stand For Examination, this command demands that your dog stand completely still while the judge takes a close look at him. Even if you do not plan to enter your dog in obedience trials, the command is a useful one. It is helpful when brushing or bathing your dog, as well as when encountering people on your daily walk.

To teach your dog to stand, put him into position any way you can–lift him or tell him to heel and stay. Place your hand under his belly as you give the command 'Stand,' exerting a mild pressure.

Above: **When your dog has mastered sit-stay on leash, practice the lesson off leash in a fenced area.**

Work in a room free of distractions. As you've seen before, your dog will be confused, so be gentle and soothing, keeping you hand under his belly as you repeat the command. Expect him to try to sit down. Just keep reassuring him as you repeat 'Stand.' End the stand, as you would any other command, with 'OK.'

Try this exercise for five minutes each day, after an outdoor training session. You can use the time for grooming. In a week's time, your dog will be standing happily and patiently.

ENOUGH. Enough is a useful command for those times that you have had enough—when your two Golden Retrievers are romping through the house. 'Enough' is the command you use to stop behavior that was acceptable up to that point. There is an important distinction between 'No' and 'Enough.' 'No' applies to forbidden activities, while 'Enough' just puts an end to something that has gotten out of hand. If you keep the difference straight, your dog will too.

To teach your dog 'Enough,' wait until one of those times when your dog has exceeded his bounds. For example, your four-month-old puppy has sounded the alarm when the door bell rings and continues to bark long after he should. In a loud, authoritative voice, tell your dog 'Enough.' Use the dog's name to get his (or her)

Above: **A woman and her Golden Retriever work on sit. Note that the trainer combines the hand signal with the verbal command.**

attention–'Amanda, enough.' Amanda (or whoever) will probably turn to look at you. If so, praise her. If your dog resumes barking, give the command again and praise him when he stops barking. If you were unable to get your dog's attention in the first place, grasp his collar and give him a good shake as you say 'Enough.' When he quiets down, praise him. If the dog continues to bark, give him a few more shakes, repeat the command, and put him in a long down for 20 minutes.

WAIT. 'Wait' is a command that is required in obedience competition in Great Britain, but it is also useful for the pet owner. Like 'Enough,' 'Wait' is a subtle command that demonstrates the dog's remarkable ability to not only learn, but to understand. 'Wait' signals a brief pause, unlike 'Stay,' which asks your dog to freeze for an undetermined time. 'Wait' can be used in an emergency–when you want your dog to stop in his tracks–or when you need to run back in to the house for a moment. 'Wait' lets your dog know that in a moment he'll have his way, that in a moment he can get out of the car, that he can soon go outside, or that he can soon dash across the park.

When you find yourself and your dog in one of those situations where you want him to wait, tell your dog in a loud voice to 'Wait.' Your tone of voice alone should be enough to make him stop and turn to look at you, at which point you will praise him for waiting. If he continues, tell him 'No, wait.' He already understands 'No' so he'll stop and after a few attempts the meaning of 'Wait' will become clear.

DISTANT CONTROL. Being able to control your dog from a distance is required for obedience trials, but it is especially handy for the pet owner who wants to have a reliable off leash dog. To teach 'Down' from a distance, put your dog in a sit stay and back away about a foot. Give the command 'Down' as you raise your right hand in the air and then sweep it down to the ground. If you are lucky your dog will obey and lie down. Tell him to 'Stay' and try the exercise again. On the other hand, he may be confused by the strange, new hand signal. In that case, step forward, and as you bring the right arm down to the ground in the down signal, grab his collar and bring him down with your hand. It may take a few attempts before your dog understands what you want him to do, but dogs are bright animals and yours will soon catch on. Once he has caught on, work with him from a distance of six feet. That way, if he slips up, you can quickly rush forward and pull him down as you give the hand signal. Continue to work with him from a distance of six feet for about a week, and then begin to vary the distance–sometimes trying it farther away and other times, closer in.

The hand signal for 'Sit' from a distance is the opposite of the signal for down. For 'Sit,' the hand is raised from the ground. The lesson is taught in much the same way, but you begin with your dog in the down stay position. Step back and tell him to sit as you raise your right hand, palm facing up. If he doesn't sit, try it again, this time pulling him into a sitting position with your signal hand. Once your dog is in the sit position, he'll be inclined to come to you, so tell him to stay.

Control from a distance requires a great deal of concentration from you and your dog and thus is very tiring, so don't overdo it. Limit yourself to no more than six attempts in one training session, and once your dog has mastered the command review it only periodically.

DROP ON RECALL. In this command, your dog is asked to come and then dropped (told to go down) when he is on his way back to you. Required in obedience trials, the command can be a lifesaver in an emergency. Imagine your dog is about to cross the street right in the path of a speeding car. If he knows the drop on recall, you have saved his life.

After your dog has learned to drop from a distance on verbal or hand signal, you can begin to teach him the drop on recall. Make your dog sit stay about 12 feet away from you. Call him to come and when he is about one third of the distance away from you, give the hand signal for down, along with the verbal command in a good, strong voice. If you are lucky, he'll drop on the spot. Wait briefly and then give both the verbal command and hand signal to come. When he comes and sits in front of you, praise him—make a big deal of it. Try it one more time before moving on to another exercise. Practice this twice a week, no more than three times a session.

If your dog does not drop when told, run to meet him and give him the drop signal. With a little patience and perseverance on your part, he'll soon catch on.

Some dogs will do fine on the drop part, but creep slowly forward when they should be joyfully returning to their masters. In this case, work on just the recall part of the exercise. One of the best ways to teach your dog to come to you is to run away from him. At the last minute turn and let him catch you, and then praise him excessively. Another method for working on the recall is to suddenly run away from the dog when he is heeling and call 'Come.' Again, let him catch you and praise him to the heavens. Make a game of it with the rest of the family by having them take turns calling the dog and, of course, wildly praising him when he comes.

OFF LEASH TRAINING. Once your dog has mastered the basic commands, you can begin training him off leash. Off leash training requires patience. If you push the dog to his limits, he'll get tired and simply walk away. What's to stop him? Until he is fully trained, your word isn't enough. Therefore, off leash training must be conducted in a safe, fenced area where your dog cannot suddenly decide that the lesson is over and dash off.

After you have found a safe place to work with your dog, begin the off leash lesson by reviewing the commands on leash. Then take off the leash and try sit, stay, down. When you made the transition from working inside with your puppy to working outside, you discovered there was a world of difference. The puppy who behaved beautifully in your living room was far too distracted to obey when exposed to the fascinating sights and sounds of the great outdoors. Likewise, the transition from on leash to off leash training is fraught with frustrations. The leash, your symbol of authority, is cast aside and your dog must obey, and, eventually, he will obey because you are the leader

Above: One way to teach your dog to come is to encourage him with enthusiastic shouts. Use the dog's name mixed with cries of 'Good Boy!' (or Girl) but give the command 'Come' *only* once. If you repeat the command, you are teaching the dog that he doesn't have to come to you the first time you call.

Above: **A trainer puts his dog in a down-stay. The hand signal—moving the palm of his hand into the dog's nose—reinforces the verbal command. Eventually, the dog should be trained to respond to either the verbal command or the hand signal.**

of the pack and he wants to please you. Now, however, his concentration is minimal; instead of learning he'll want to run and play, so keep the lessons short at first. That way you'll both end the day with a feeling of accomplishment. End the training session by letting your dog romp around outdoors, off leash.

The next day make the lesson a little longer, perhaps asking your dog to stay down for two minutes instead of one. In a few days, try heeling off the leash, but only if he really knows how to heel on leash. Does he stop automatically when you do? Does he walk readily and patiently by your side? If you need to tug your dog into place as you heel, he's not ready for off leash heeling. When you are ready to work on off leash heeling, begin by heeling on leash. Then simply support the leash in the open palm off your left hand, letting the rest of the leash drag behind you. If your dog starts to wander off or lag behind, all you need to do is grasp the leash and bring him back into place. For the moment, keep control of the leash. After a minute or two of heeling on leash, again try the open palm method. End the day with playtime.

When the two of you are making progress with the leash held in your palm, move on to the next phase of off leash training. As you are walking, drop the leash. If your dog starts to run off, you can stop him by stepping on the leash. For peace of mind, you know you have the added security of the fence, which will stop him if he takes a mad

dash. If your dog is still a puppy, you'll want to continue working with the dropped leash for awhile. Even though all seems to be going well, chances are he'll bolt as soon as the leash is unsnapped.

Off leash training is an ongoing process. If you started when the dog was a puppy you've laid valuable groundwork. The goal of off leash training is to make your dog as reliable off leash as he is on leash. As your puppy grows older, add new lessons as you continue with off leash training.

For safety's sake, work your dog in the enclosed area until you feel confident that your dog will behave. Two tools will help you through this stage of training: a long training leash, roughly 10 to 12 feet, to use as a drop line and a tab—a very short leash that works as a handle. It allows you to exert control over your dog even though he is off the

Above: Once your dog has mastered sit, you can work on stay. As you give the command to stay, along with the hand signal, slowly back away from your dog. Gradually increase the distance between you and your dog, as well as the time you require him to stay.

Above: To train your dog to stay, walk away from him, around him, even over him. He must learn not to move until you give him the okay.

leash. It also acts as a *reminder* of your control. The presence of the tab reminds your dog that you are the boss.

Use the drop line in the same way you used the leash when working on off leash heel. Because the drop leash is longer than a regular leash, it may take awhile for your dog to get used to the feeling of it dragging behind him.

Alternate between the drop line and the short tab when practicing heeling off leash. During the first month of serious off leash training, continue to work on the basic commands as well as more advanced commands, such as drop on recall, when not working on heel. Work on 'Come' and 'Stay' from a greater distance. After about a month's time, you should feel pleased with your dog's performance— and yours, too. Using the drop line, you should be ready to take him out on the street to work on heel. Work in as secluded an area as possible to avoid traffic as well as people who might step on the line. There are bound to be distractions that may break your dog's concentration, but if he gets out of line you still have control with your drop line. Keep the first street lesson short, increasing the time gradually as both of you gain confidence. In another month, you should be ready to try the short tab.

You may never want to let your dog off the leash while walking down a busy city street, but it's reassuring to know that your dog *is* trained to walk by your side. If you live in an area where traffic is minimal, both you and your dog will enjoy the freedom of off leash heeling.

RETRIEVE. Some dogs, especially retrievers, will naturally bring a thrown object back to their owners. Training reinforces this natural tendency, while teaching the dog that there is a proper time for everything. The untrained dog may have no problem with fetching a ball, but he may want to play fetch while you are trying to read the Sunday paper; conversely, he may decide to chew on the ball rather than return it to you when you throw it.

To teach a dog to fetch, throw a ball or stick and call out 'Fetch.' Your dog will naturally run after it. If the dog doesn't return with the object, command it to 'Come.' If the dog prefers romping around with the object, a long leash to pull the dog to you will come in handy. Shower your dog with praise when he returns. Tell him to 'Sit' and take the object from his mouth. If the dog resists your removing the object, grasp his upper jaw, telling him 'Let Go.' 'Fetch' is fun, as well as useful, because it a good way to give your dog the exercise he needs.

Retrieving is an important part of obedience trials. Dogs must retrieve dumbbells, sometimes as part of a hurdle-jumping exercise, and in the advanced classes must retrieve a specific object.

SCENT DISCRIMINATION. In the Utility Class of AKC obedience trials, a dog must find an object that belongs to his handler. To teach a dog how to do this exercise, you'll need a group of volunteers. Everyone should place an article of theirs (such as a glove) on the ground. Without your dog seeing it, you should place one of your belongings on the floor with the other articles after handling it several times to give it your scent.

Lead your dog among the objects saying 'Seek.' If he picks up your object, praise him, but if he passes it by lead him back to it and give him the object. If your dog tries to pick up another object, firmly tell him 'No.' Try the exercise several times, using different articles until he learns that he must pick up only those with your scent.

Once he has learned to find your article, teach him to bring it to you in the way he would retrieve a ball—to sit in front of you so that you can take the object. In competition, the dog must finish the exercise in the heel position.

Though this may seem like an exercise that has no use for the average pet owner, your dog can be taught to find an article that you have misplaced.

TRAINING THE PROBLEM DOG

The key to training the so-called problem dog is to understand the reason behind the behavior. By understanding the cause of the behavior, you'll have a better chance to modify the behavior.

BITING DOGS. Most dogs bite out of fear. Since many dog bites are inflicted against children, when possible you can attempt to modify the behavior of children as well as that of the dog. Tell your children and the neighborhood children not to run up to the dog. They should never extend their fingers to the dog, but instead should show the dog a clenched fist. To help the dog overcome its fearful aggression, you need to desensitize the dog. If your dog always barks

Above: 'Shake hands' is an easy and fun trick to teach your dog. Like anything else, your dog will learn this trick through repetition. Lift your dog's paw as you say 'Shake hands.' After several attempts, your dog will understand what you want him to do.

Below: Playtime is important, too, and should not be neglected while you are training your dog.

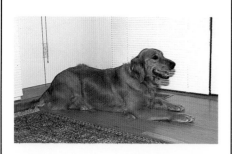

Above: The long down can be used as a discipline tool. In fact, to reinforce your role as the 'leader of the pack' it is a good practice to make your dog stay in a long down for at least five minutes every day.

Facing page: This woman and her dog have a good relationship. The dog wants to please and the woman is consistent in her commands.

at and tries to bite strangers, you need to teach the dog not to be afraid. To do this, you will need a friend to help you. Have your helper face the dog from a safe distance and reward non-aggressive behavior with praise or food. With each training session, reduce the distance between the dog and the feared object. Always reward good behavior with praise and punish bad behavior by ignoring the dog. Any sort of attention, even punishment by scolding, may reinforce the bad behavior.

Above all, *train your dog.* A professional trainer is probably the best solution. A command from the owner can avert trouble, even when dealing with an aggressive dog. In addition, increase the amount of exercise he receives and have correctional aids on hand. Water dumped on the head, or a squirt of lemon juice in the face, will put out the fire of a snarling dog.

SEPARATION ANXIETY. Some dogs have extreme reactions to being left alone. They bark and whine in your absence, chew objects to the point of destruction and urinate and defecate in the house. Most puppies experience some form of anxiety when first left alone, but in most cases they become used to being left alone. Avoid major problems by handling the situation when the dog is young. Having a regular routine helps to ease the problem. Every dog needs an area of his own, whether it is a dog run or a corner of the kitchen. Train your puppy to 'Go to sleep' at a natural time to do so—after eating or playing—and put him in his special area. When you leave the puppy alone, he should be ready to sleep and will come to associate being left alone with going to sleep. If possible, a quick walk around the block will help to make him feel more relaxed. To combat destructive chewing, give your dog plenty of distractions—rubber toys, rawhide chews. Don't draw attention to your departure with a lengthy farewell. Instead, leave with a quick and upbeat good-bye.

DESTRUCTIVENESS. A young puppy will chew while he is teething—there's no way to combat nature. But you can make sure he won't destroy any of your belongings by giving him lots of toys to chew on *and* by preventing him from getting his sharp little teeth on the rungs of your grandmother's oak chair. A young puppy should not be given the run of the house. When you cannot watch him, put him in his crate. If a corner of the kitchen is the puppy's home while you are at work, clear out the corner so there's nothing that he can damage and be sure to give him his toys. Granted, it may be inconvenient to move your kitchen table out of the kitchen, but it's only a temporary inconvenience.

In the meantime, reprimand your puppy with a stern 'No' every time he does start chewing on an inappropriate object. Then give him something he can chew on—a rawhide chew or a safe toy—and tell him 'OK.' In a few months, nature will have run its course—the urge to chew will have diminished—and you will have trained your puppy not to eat your shoes.

But what about the adult dog that chews? Dogs chew because they are bored, so give your adult dogs toys, too. Make sure that your dog is getting plenty of exercise. If you leave him alone for long hours, think about hiring a neighborhood kid to walk him while you

Above: With this crew of kids, teaching Dusty not to beg is nearly impossible!

Right: Dogs should not be allowed to jump up on people. This is a bad habit that is often difficult to break because you are fighting your dog's friendly nature and enthusiasm for meeting people.

When your dog jumps up, push her down, telling her 'Sit' or 'Down,' and then praise her when she obeys.

are at work. At the very least, take your dog for a walk or have a rousing game of fetch as soon as you get home from work.

Digging is another strong, natural impulse, and if you don't want holes in your yard, a compromise is probably the best solution. In other words, you take one half of the yard and the dog takes the other. When you are outside, your dog can enjoy the run of the entire yard, along with the pleasure of your company, because you are there to stop him from tearing up the rose bushes that your husband so thoughtfully gave you for your birthday. But when you are inside, the dog goes back to his half of the yard.

FEAR OF LOUD NOISES. Many dogs are frightened by loud noises— anything from vacuum cleaners and hair dryers to fireworks and thunder. You can help your dog overcome his fear by getting him accustomed to other loud noises. For example, drop a book on the floor and then speak to the dog reassuringly. With a young dog, at the first sign of fear, reassure it before the fear develops into a phobia, but be careful the reassurance doesn't become a positive reward in itself.

Left: **Do not allow your dog to pull on the leash. Try to keep the leash slack so that you can use the choke collar to keep the dog in line.** *Above:* **A Golden Retriever, at nine weeks.**

SHYNESS. A shy or timid dog may not seem like a problem, but it is. Whether in a person or a dog, shyness is painful. The causes of shyness are many. It can be the result of careless breeding or lack of exposure to people and activities while young. Training is essential to help your dog overcome shyness. If your dog is trained to heel, he cannot hide behind you if you encounter something spooky on your walk. If your dog does cower behind you, don't try to soothe it with comforting words. Your dog will interpret your words as praise for its timid behavior. Instead, praise the dog when he doesn't act timidly—when he ventures down a new street, for example.

URINATING IN THE HOUSE. In some cases of this behavior, the dog may be attempting to mask another scent, such as perfume or tobacco, so you will need to remove the source. In other cases, the problem may be hormonal. Male dogs mark their territory with urine, and a female dog uses her urine to tell males she is available. In these situations, your first approach should be to go through the steps for housebreaking again. If that fails, talk to your vet about neutering the animal. If you cannot determine the cause of the problem, consult your vet—improper elimination may have its roots in a physical disorder.

JUMPING UP. Dogs jump up because they are excited to see you. To break your dog of this bad habit, firmly tell him 'No' and then give him the command 'Sit' or 'Down.' Go down to the dog's level and praise him and pet him. Praise your dog every time he greets you on all fours.

Above: **Part of your dog's training should include learning to socialize with other dogs.**

Facing page: **When your dog has mastered basic obedience, you can teach him to do tricks. This Poodle is being taught to climb a ladder.**

BEGGING. Reprimand your dog if he begs for food, and *never* give in and feed him from the dinner table; otherwise, he'll know that with a little perseverance, he'll get what he wants. Feeding your dog before you eat will help eliminate his urge to beg for food from your dinner.

TEACHING YOUR DOG TO DO TRICKS

Some people don't see the point of teaching their dogs to do tricks and in fact don't approve because it seems cruel. But as long as your dog is having fun, there's no harm done.

When your dog has mastered the essential commands of sit, stay, come, heel and down, you can move on to other, more amusing, commands: 'Give me your paw,' 'Roll over' and the like. The principles for obedience training apply to any sort of training:

1. Keep the training sessions short.

Above: **A grounding in basic obedience is important before you can teach roll over. Your dog needs to understand down so you can manipulate him into the proper position. Above all, your dog must understand the concept of learning something new.**

Facing page: **The Poodle seen on page 31 has learned to climb the ladder. Now his trainer is teaching him to stay when he reaches the top of the ladder.**

2. Show your dog what you want it to do. They don't speak English, so you need to manipulate them into the correct position.
3. Praise your dog when he performs the command.
4. Work on only one command at a time.

SHAKE. Begin the lesson by telling the dog to sit. Take one of your dog's paws (always use the same one) in your hand while repeating the command 'Shake.' Dogs instinctively lift a paw during play, so this action is not as strange as it may seem. In fact, the next time your dog paws you during a game, you can turn a play session into a quick lesson by grabbing his paw as you say 'Shake. Good boy.' With some dogs, a biscuit encourages the movement, but some will simply be distracted by the food. Be sure to reinforce the action with lavish praise.

ROLL OVER. 'Roll over' is more difficult to learn. To teach your dog to roll over, tell it to lie down and then take it through the motions of rolling over while repeating 'Roll over.' Moving your hand in a circling motion provides a good visual signal.

SPEAK. To teach your dog to bark on command, cash in on one of those moments when he'll bark naturally, such as when the doorbell rings. As an alternative you can try barking yourself in order to start him barking. When he does bark, say 'Speak. Good dog.' When he starts barking on command, combine the command with pointing at him. Alternate the verbal command with the point and in a short time your dog bark on a hand signal alone. 'So what?' you might ask. For starters, you can amuse your friends, but you can also give yourself an added sense of security by knowing that your dog will bark when you point at him. Suppose you hear a noise outside. If there is someone lurking about, a barking dog is more intimidating sounding than a woman saying 'Speak.'

Dogs can be trained to be the eyes for the blind *(above)* and the ears for the deaf *(below)*.

Labradors, Golden Retrievers and German Shepherds are the most commonly used breeds for seeing eye, or guide, dogs. Training begins when the dogs are only eight weeks old. They spend a year with a volunteer who teaches them basic obedience and social skills. Afterwards, they go through intensive guide dog training.

Hearing ear dogs alert their owners to ringing telephones, doorbells, alarm clocks, whistling tea kettles and crying babies. These dogs can be any breed and are often rescued from humane societies.

Facing page: Trainers Cary Voorhees and Carole Anderson of Dogs For The Deaf with Wiggles and Amy.

SHOWING YOUR DOG

Above: **The Bichon Frisé is growing in popularity in the United States and was recognized by the AKC in 1988.**

Facing page: **This young girl has high hopes for her Chihuahua at this international dog show held in Mexico City.**

INTRODUCTION

The first dog shows were held in England in the 1830s. One authority has suggested that these low-key events were a result of the ban on dog fighting and bull baiting. Following the ban, dog fanciers channeled their competitive energies in a less barbarous direction, and dog shows were born in the local pubs and taverns. The first official dog show took place at Newcastle-upon-Tyne, England in 1859. The first field trial was held six years later at Southill in Bedfordshire. As might be expected with any competition, judges and breeders disagreed over what constituted a winning dog. Thus, The Kennel Club was organized by British dog fanciers to impose order on the new sport. Rules and regulations governing shows, as well as breed standards, were eventually developed. Today, The Kennel Club of England recognizes over 180 breeds of dogs.

As enthusiasm for dogs spread through the British Empire, western Europe, and North America, dog shows and organizations naturally followed. The first dog show in the United States was held in 1874 in Mineola, New York. Three years later the Westminster Kennel Club in New York held its first show, featuring 1201 dogs. The show has been an annual event since then.

By 1884, dog fanciers in the United States, like those in Britain, saw the need for an umbrella organization and established the American Kennel Club to sponsor shows and promote the welfare of purebred dogs. The AKC is today composed of 446 autonomous dog clubs, registers over one million dogs a year, and has records for more than 34,509,798 dogs dating back to 1878.

Although the American Kennel Club is the largest and best known organization in the United States, there are smaller clubs, too, such as the United Kennel Club and Worldwide Kennel Club.

The United Kennel Club is guided by the 'total dog' concept. Chauncey Z Bennet, who founded the UKC in 1898, was concerned that dogs were being bred for looks at the expense of their working instincts. The UKC has continued to follow his philosophy, and most of the dogs they register today perform the tasks for which the breed was originally bred.

Above: **Off to the show! Be sure to have a cage or crate for your dog and his supplies: food, water, bowls, grooming utensils, show leash and a few treats. You might also want to bring a lawn chair to sit in while waiting for your event.**

About the time the AKC was formed, the need for a similar organization was gaining momentum in Canada. On 27 September 1888, the Canadian Kennel Club (CKC) was established at Tecumseh House in London, Ontario. The first of the 350 dogs registered that year was an English Setter named Forest Fern. Today, the CKC registers approximately 70,000 dogs per year and recognizes over 300 breeds of dogs. Every year the CKC holds over 1500 shows and trials.

The term 'dog show' generally refers to a bench competition, so named because the dogs are exhibited on a platform or bench. The judging takes place in a ring, where judges assess the dog while he is in motion and standing still. The dog is judged on the basis of appearance, physique, bearing and temperament according to the breed standard—a description of a perfect specimen of the breed. A standard is quite detailed, discussing everything from the color of the nose to the size of the tail, from how the dog moves to its expression. A deviation from the standard is considered a fault. Thus, a fault could be physical, such as legs that are too long, or temperamental, such as hostility or timidity in the ring. The standard serves as a guide for judges and breeders alike.

Today, the Westminster Dog Show in New York is the most prestigious championship dog show in the United States. Crufts, established in 1886, is the major show in England. Entry to these shows is

limited to dogs that have won the required certificates at other championship shows.

Showing a dog involves a lot of time and effort. Because success in the ring depends to a large extent on the dog's appearance, your dog has to be carefully groomed and in top physical condition–an ongoing responsibility. For long-haired dogs especially, a show represents a culmination of months of grooming.

Your dog must also be up-to-date on all his shots. Wherever there are large groups of animals together, the risk of disease is greater. Outbreaks of kennel cough can often be linked to a show.

Of course the dog must be well-trained. He must know how to move well in the ring (and so should the owner), and he must feel comfortable around hundreds (in some cases, thousands) of people and other dogs.

In spite of the work involved, a dog show is fun, for spectators as well as exhibitors. Everyone is there because they love dogs. The spectators enjoy looking at all the different kinds of breeds, and many people will not be able to resist petting the dogs. A few people will get so carried away they will even hug and kiss the dogs. A friendly camaraderie exists between the dog owners, and of course the winners feel jubilant with their dogs' performance. In many ways, a dog show is a social event, complete with lots of food and champagne.

Above: Waiting for the action to begin at a local dog show in California.

Above: **Spectators and participants wander around 'backstage' at the local dog show. Smaller events such as these are a good place for beginners to learn the ropes.** *Right:* **Welsh Pembroke Corgis being gaited in the ring.**

Facing page: **A Standard Poodle is measured to see that he fits within the breed standard. The Standard Poodle must be over 15 inches at the highest point of the shoulder.**

Most dogs enjoy shows, too. Dogs like nothing better than to be with their owners and feel especially happy when they sense their owners' pleasure. Moreover, many dogs thrive on the attention from all the spectators. Some dogs, however, do start to feel stressed after a full day of competition.

DOG SHOW PROCEDURE

To enter a purebred dog in a show, the dog must first be registered. If you would like to enter your pedigreed dog in a dog show, your local breed society can advise you about upcoming shows and the proper procedure for entering. The application for the show must be made several weeks in advance. You will need to specify the class in which you wish to enter your dog. (The various classes are explained below.) Before the show, you will receive an entry ticket and a benching number (for benched shows).

When you arrive at the show, first of all pick up the catalog. It will contain everything a handler needs to know, especially the order in which the classes will be judged. The first class will be the only one with a definite time, but the others will follow according to the numbered order. Be sure to watch the judges' table for the number indicating which class is currently being judged.

After you have picked up the catalog, get your dog situated at his bench, making sure he is comfortable. Having his own bed or

Above: Gaiting in the ring. A handler must keep a close eye on the dog at all times to ensure that he moves at the right pace. Notice that the handler is wearing comfortable shoes. The handler cannot allow his movements to hinder the dog.

blanket gives the dog a sense of security. Give him a drink of water, but withhold food until after he has been shown to avoid a sleepy-looking dog in the ring.

You will need to bring along various supplies:
• grooming equipment (combs, brushes, scissors, dry shampoo, polishing spray
• the dog's bed and blanket
• drinking bowl and bottle of water (in case water is not readily available)
• food and feeding bowl
• benching chain (to secure the dog to his stall)
• show leash, usually nylon or leather
• dog treats

Exercise areas will have been set aside so that you can run through a rehearsal with your dog. Trial and error will determine when and how much to rehearse. Aside from rehearsing, you should keep your dog at his bench until right before he enters the ring. That way, he will be more alert and move briskly about the ring. A dog that has been standing around waiting for his turn tends to get bored and won't perform as well.

The handler's mood can help or hinder the dog's performance. If the handler is nervous or apprehensive, the dog will sense that, and his performance may be off. A confident handler makes for a confident dog, and a dog that is an old hand at showing will know to put on his best performance as he steps into the ring.

Judging begins with all the dogs in a class being gaited around the ring. This allows the judge to examine the class as a whole and also allows the dogs and handlers the chance to loosen up a bit. When moving in line with other dogs and handlers, make sure that your dog has plenty of room to move so that his gait will not be thrown off.

The way your dog moves is one of his most important characteristics. A dog should move freely and with confidence, and a dog and handler should move as one, in a seemingly effortless manner. In reality, like any skill, learning how to gait a dog requires practice. Before a dog is ready for a show, the owner/handler will have spent hours practicing and experimenting to find the proper speed and length of leash. An experienced observer can help you find the right pace.

On the day of the show, the handler can take steps to aid a dog's performance. Since the handler is moving briskly about the ring, he or she should wear comfortable clothing and shoes. Large dogs require a fast pace and a handler that is struggling to keep up will throw off the dog's pace. Once in the ring, the handler must keep a close eye on the dog to ensure that he is moving at the proper pace. It is also up to the handler to pick a clean and level route for the dog to run. A small clump of dirt can hamper a smooth run.

After the dogs have been gaited around the ring as a class, many judges like to walk down the line to gain an overall impression of balance, type and quality. The judge will then examine each dog individually, asking each handler to present the stand. To arrange your dog in the proper position, place one hand under the dog's chest to raise the front end, and then run the hand up the neck to put

Left: A woman and her Golden Retriever practice gaiting. It may take a lot of practice before you and your dog can move smoothly as a team. *Above:* During a show, a break between events gives this trainer and her Samoyed time to rehearse.

the head in its proper position. With the other hand, adjust the legs and tail. All of this should be done as quickly as possible. It should look as if you are petting the dog rather than arranging it. Avoid putting your hand under the dog's belly, as this may cause the dog to arch his back, and be careful not to position the hind legs too far apart or else the front legs will bend and the back will dip.

Like gaiting, the stand takes practice. Some owners begin training their puppies by putting them in the proper position every day from the time they are eight weeks old. Practice the stand in front of a mirror so you can review the results.

When your dog is in the stand, the judge will examine him from head to toe. A dog will be judged on his general demeanor, stance and presence, with his poise playing a large part in his success. A dog should stand patiently and proudly as the judge examines him. Using the breed standard as his guide, the judge evaluates the dog's color, size and so forth as specified by the standard. He will determine if the dog has any disqualifying faults. A Golden Retriever, for example, can be disqualified if he is too tall or too short. A dog that has been disqualified by three different judges may not be shown again.

The judge will also assess the gait of each dog individually, reviewing the dog as he moves from one side of the ring to the other, as well as when he is coming toward and going away from him. When moving toward or away from the judge, the dog should move at a slower pace than when moving from side to side. It is extremely important that the dog move in a straight line. Though some people make gaiting look easy, there are others who find themselves getting tangled up with their dogs, so don't be discouraged if, at first, you and your dog don't perform as well as you would have liked. With a little perseverance, the two of you can look like pros.

Above: St Bernards line up for the judge. Males and females compete separately and then the winners compete against each other.

Facing page: A woman and her Cocker Spaniel. The texture of the coat is very important. It should be silky and either flat or slightly wavy. A coat that is too curly or has a cottony texture will be penalized.

RULES AND REGULATIONS OF A DOG SHOW

Dog clubs throughout the world have established rules and regulations governing the showing of dogs. In the United States, for example, the American Kennel Club is the main governing body. Established in 1884, the main functions of the AKC are to protect and advance purebred dogs; promote and improve dog shows and field, working and obedience trials; grant licenses to dog shows; give awards; classify breeds; and register pedigreed dogs.

For a dog to compete in an AKC show, he must be a purebred, registered dog. The American Kennel club recognizes 130 breeds, which are divided into the seven groups listed below.

Above: The Clumber Spaniel is a long, low, heavy dog. His expression is pensive, but he shows great enthusiasm for both work and play. *Right:* Champion Sundance's Southlake Legend, a prizewinning Labrador Retriever owned by Joyce and Jim Woods.

Group 1: Sporting Dogs

Brittanys
Pointers
Pointers (German Shorthaired)
Pointers (German Wirehaired)
Retrievers (Chesapeake Bay)
Retrievers (Curly-Coated)
Retrievers (Flat-Coated)
Retrievers (Golden)
Retrievers (Labrador)
Setters (English)
Setters (Gordon)
Setters (Irish)
Spaniels (American Water)
Spaniels (Clumber)
Spaniels (Cocker)
Spaniels (English Cocker)
Spaniels (Field)
Spaniels (Irish Water)
Spaniels (Sussex)
Vizslas
Weimaraners
Wirehaired Pointing Griffons

Group 2: Hounds
Afghan Hounds
Basenjis
Basset Hounds
Beagles
Black and Tan Coonhounds
Bloodhounds
Borzois
Dachshunds
Foxhounds (American)
Foxhounds (English)
Greyhounds
Harriers
Ibizan Hounds
Irish Wolfhounds
Norwegian Elkhounds
Otterhounds
Pharaoh Hounds
Rhodesian Ridgebacks
Salukis
Scottish Deerhounds
Whippets

Group 3: Working Dogs
Akitas
Alaskan Malamutes
Bernese Mountain Dogs
Boxers
Bullmastiffs
Doberman Pinschers
Giant Schnauzers
Great Danes
Great Pyrenees
Komondorok
Mastiffs
Newfoundlands
Portuguese Water Dogs
Rottweilers
St Bernards
Samoyeds
Siberian Huskies
Standard Schnauzers

Above: To show off the breed's graceful form, an Afghan must be moved quickly around the ring. *Left:* Tom Joyner and his Rottweiller, Beamer. Tom is beginning off leash training with Beamer. Note that he has the leash tucked in his pocket rather than in his hand.

Above: **As described by the AKC, the Bulldog's 'disposition should be equable and kind, resolute and courageous (not vicious or aggressive), and demeanor should be pacific and dignified.'**

Right: **A small dog, weighing roughly 12 to 15 pounds, the Border Terrier is good-tempered, obedient and easily trained.**

Group 4: Terriers

Airedale Terriers	Lakeland Terriers
American Staffordshire Terriers	Manchester Terriers
Australian Terriers	Miniature Schnauzers
Bedlington Terriers	Norfolk Terriers
Border Terriers	Norwich Terriers
Bull Terriers	Scottish Terriers
Cairn Terriers	Sealyham Terriers
Dandie Dinmont Terriers	Skye Terriers
Fox Terriers (Smooth)	Soft Coated Wheaten Terriers
Fox Terriers (Wire)	Staffordshire Bull Terriers
Irish Terriers	Welsh Terriers
Kerry Blue Terriers	West Highland White Terriers

Group 5: Toys
  Affenpinschers
  Brussels Griffons
  Chihuahuas
  English Toy Spaniels
  Italian Greyhounds
  Japanese Chin
  Maltese
  Manchester Terriers
  Miniature Pinschers
  Papillons
  Pinschers
  Pekingese
  Pomeranians
  Poodles

  Pugs
  Shih Tzu
  Silky Terriers
  Yorkshire Terriers

Group 6:
Non-Sporting Dogs
  Bichon Frisés
  Boston Terriers
  Bulldogs
  Chow Chows
  Dalmatians
  Finnish Spitz
  French Bulldogs
  Keeshonden
  Lhasa Apsos
  Poodles
  Schipperkes
  Tibetan Spaniels
  Tibetan Terriers

Above: The Pomeranian, a member of the toy group, is an alert dog with an intelligent expression. The ideal show specimen should weigh from four to five pounds.

Certain breeds that have not gained full recognition from the American Kennel Club can participate in AKC shows in the Miscellaneous Class only. These breeds are:

Australian Kelpies
Border Collies
Canaan Dog
Chinese Cresteds
Chinese Shar-Peis
Cavalier King Charles Spaniels
Finnish Spitz
Greater Swiss Mountain Dogs
Miniature Bull Terriers
Petit Basset Griffon Vendeen
Spinoni Italiani

All of these breeds can be shown together in a single class, or a separate class can be offered for any of the individual breeds. In order for a dog to compete in the Miscellaneous Class, the owner must apply for an Indefinite Listing Privilege (ILP). These dogs are not eligible for competition beyond the Miscellaneous Class, but they may compete in obedience trials.

Breed societies have established breed standards for these dogs, and, typically, as a breed grows in popularity, recognition by the American Kennel Club soon follows. There are exceptions, however. The Miniature Bull Terrier, for example, has had a loyal following for over 80 years but has remained in the Miscellaneous Class since 1963.

Group 7: Herding Dogs

Australian Cattle Dogs	Collies
Bearded Collies	German Shepherd Dogs
Belgian Malinois	Old English Sheepdogs
Belgian Sheepdogs	Pulik
Belgian Tervuren	Shetland Sheepdogs
Bouviers des Flandres	Welsh Corgis (Cardigan)
Briards	Welsh Corgis (Pembroke)

The breed categories in the United Kingdom are much the same as they are in the United States, with a few exceptions. In the United Kingdom, the Non-sporting group is known as the Utility group. Within the groups, there are a few differences as well. The Bichon Frise, for example, belongs to the Non-sporting group in the United States, but to the Toy group in the United Kingdom. In addition, some breeds are recognized in one country but not in others. The Kennel Club of England recognized the Border Collie in 1976, while in the United States the breed has not yet achieved AKC

Dogs from the herding group are used in a number of capacities far beyond the purpose for which they were originally bred. German Shepherds *(above)* are part of the Armed Forces. Collies are television and movie stars, as illustrated by this still from MGM's *Lassie Come Home (left)*. Herding dogs also make wonderful pets. The photo *on the far left* shows Queen Elizabeth as a child, with her beloved Corgis.

recognition. Clubs in the same countries don't necessarily recognize the same breeds. The United Kennel Club of the United States recognizes the Boykin Spaniel, but the American Kennel Club does not recognize the breed.

The AKC also requires that a dog must be disease free and intact (neither spayed or castrated). Though not eligible for championship points, neutered dogs may compete in nonregular classes and in obedience trials.

According to the rules of the American Kennel Club, there are four types of shows: member, licensed, specialty and sanctioned match. Member shows are given by a club or association that is a member of the American Kennel Club. Licensed shows are given by clubs or associations that do not belong to the AKC, but have been granted permission to hold that particular show. Both of these types of shows award championship points.

A specialty show is given by a club or association that was formed to improve a particular breed. An American-bred specialty show limits entry to American-bred dogs only. Specialty shows also award championship points.

Above: After weeks of training, a Chow Chow is ready for his first show. Some trainers begin putting their puppies in a stand as early as eight weeks old.

Sanctioned match shows are less intense forms of competition, as they do not award championship points and are therefore a good starting point for the amateur dog handler. Member or licensed all-breed shows can, with AKC approval, hold shows that restrict entry to a specific class, such as for puppies or for dogs that are Champions of Record of the AKC. Championship shows are divided into classes, first by breed and then by age and handicap:

1. The Puppy Class is for dogs between six months and one year of age that are not champions.

2. The Twelve-to-Eighteen Month classes are judged only at specialty shows held separately from all-breed events. This class is for dogs between 12 and 18 months of age that are not champions.

3. The Novice Class is for dogs over six months old, whelped in the United States or Canada, which have not yet won three first prizes in the Novice Class, a first prize in Bred-by-Exhibitor, American-bred, or Open classes, nor any points toward their championships.

4. The Bred-by-Exhibitor Class is for dogs six months of age and over that are not champions. The dogs must have been whelped in the United States, or if whelped in Canada, must be individually

registered in the American Kennel Club Stud Book. Dogs in this class must be owned wholly or in part by the breeder(s) of record or by the breeder's spouse, and must be handled by the breeder or a member of his or her immediate family.

5. The American-bred Class is for all dogs, except champions, six months of age and over that were whelped in the United States.

6. The Open Class is for dogs six months of age and over.

Males and females are judged separately in each of the above classes, and then the first prize winners compete against each other, with the winner of each sex awarded Winners Dog or Winners Bitch. The winning dog also earns points that count toward the title of Champion. A Reserve Winners is also chosen.

The Winners Dog and the Winners Bitch compete against any champions entered in the show and a Best of Breed or Best of Variety of Breed is selected. (Collies, for example, have two varieties: smooth and rough.) After the Best of Breed or Best of Variety of Breed has been chosen, the Winners Dog and Winners Bitch compete for Best of Winners.

Once the Best of Breed and Best of Variety of Breed have been chosen, the judges turn their attention to the dogs of the opposite

Above: **A judge reviews a class of West Highland White Terrier puppies. After reviewing each dog, the judge offered encouraging words and advice to each of the trainers.**

Above and right: **All their hard work and effort has paid off as these owners, trainers and their dogs are awarded Best of Winners.**

sex and select a Best of Opposite Sex to Best of Breed and Best of Opposite Sex to Best of Variety of Breed. The dogs that may compete for this award are from the following categories:

1. A dog of the opposite sex from the winner of the Best of Breed.

2. The dog awarded Winners of the opposite sex to the Best of Breed or Best of Variety.

3. Any undefeated dogs of the opposite sex to the Best of Breed or Best of Variety of Breed that have competed at the show only in additional non-regular classes.

Next, the Best of Group is chosen from the Best of Breed winners in each of the seven groups (Sporting, Working, etc). These seven dogs are then judged against each other and one dog is awarded Best in Show.

A dog becomes a Champion of Record by earning 15 points, of which six or more points were won at two shows under two different judges. The balance of the points must be won under two other judges. The number of points given per show varies by show, but is explained in the catalog for that particular show.

United Kennel Club conformation shows are divided into the following classes: Puppy, for dogs six months to under one year old; Junior, for dogs one year and under two years old; Senior, for dogs two years and under three years old; and Veteran, for dogs over three years old. Males and females are judged separately, with the winners in each class competing for Best Male and Female of Show. Best of Show is chosen from the Best Male and Female of Show. Champions compete against only champions, grand champions against grand champions. Males and females are shown together at the champion level.

Above: After their event, a group of participants compare notes about their dogs' performances. The blonde woman with the hand over her face is bemoaning the fact that her dog never fails to perform perfectly at home. In the ring, however, his performance was not up to par—an experience shared by many trainers.

Left: Two Gordon Setters in the bench area. The trainers are free to decorate their benches with ribbons and other ornaments.

GROOMING YOUR DOG

Grooming is important for all dogs, but especially for show dogs. Although grooming areas are available at shows for last minute trimming and fluffing, grooming a show dog is an ongoing process.

Because the different breeds have such a wide variety of coat types, some dogs are obviously easier to care for than others. Old English Sheepdogs, Collies and Afghan Hounds clearly require more grooming time than the sleek-haired Beagle. As much as an hour a day is needed to thoroughly groom the thick coat of the Old English Sheepdog.

Grooming necessities include combs, brushes, and scissors. Select a brush that is appropriate for your dog's coat, making sure that the bristles are long enough to reach through the coat. Wide-toothed combs are handy for breaking up mats and tangles, while fine-toothed combs separate the undercoat, bringing out the dead hair. Fine-toothed combs are useful under the chin and tail and behind the ears and are a necessity during flea season. As you comb your dog, you can catch the offending fleas and then drown them in a cup of water.

To groom a long-haired dog with an undercoat (Collie, Newfoundland), use your wide-toothed comb on the tangles. Brush and

SPECIAL TECHNIQUES FOR GROOMING A SHOW DOG— WHAT'S ALLOWED AND WHAT'S NOT

A show dog's appearance is crucial for success in the ring. Carefully grooming your dog year round is an absolute necessity, but once the day of the show has arrived, a handler has a few tricks of the trade at his disposal. For example, a dog's stand can be improved by placing his forelegs on a slight hump in the ground, thereby lifting up the front end.

One trick to improve the coat of a short-haired dog, especially a dark-haired one, is to polish the dog. First, rub down the coat with a damp chamois to bring out any loose hair. Next, polish the dog with a soft fabric, such as a piece of silk or velvet, and apply a specially formulated spray to add a final finish. Your dog will now have an extra-healthy gleam to his coat.

Unfortunately, some trainers resort to illegal procedures as well. In the past, handlers have used a number of practices to alter a show dog's appearance.

(continued on page 58)

comb the coat forward over the head and shoulders before combing it back. Brush the flanks following the lay of the coat. You will need a brush with long, wide-set bristles. If possible, bathe these dogs only twice a year.

Dogs with long, silky coats, such as Afghans, Yorkies and spaniels, need frequent brushing to avoid matting. Be sure to use a brush with long bristles, or you'll end up grooming only the outer coat. These dogs require more frequent baths than other long-haired dogs.

Wire-haired dogs (most terriers) need regular combing to avoid mats. They should be stripped or plucked every three to four months, and for this you will need a stripping or plucking comb. An easier method is to have the dog professionally clipped by a groomer.

Short-haired dogs are the easiest to groom. For dogs with a short, fine coat, like a Boxer, all you will need is a 'hound glove.' Dogs with a slightly longer coat (Labrador, Golden Retriever) will need combing and brushing. A slicker brush (a rectangular brush with bent, wire bristles) is an ideal tool for removing the dead hair of the undercoat.

Curly-coated dogs require clipping every six weeks or so. A puppy's first clip will be needed at about 14 weeks. Comb and brush the coat every few days.

Far left: A groomer trims a Poodle. *Left:* Daily grooming, particularly during shedding season, is a must. A slicker brush is especially good for removing loose hairs from the undercoat. *Above:* Grooming completed, a handsome Golden Retriever is ready for the ring.

Use blunt-edged scissors to trim your dog's hair in delicate places. On occasion, you will need to trim the hair around the eyes of your Old English Sheepdog or Maltese. Spaniels need trimming between the pads of their feet and on their ear flaps to prevent hair from blocking the ear canal. In some cases, you will want to trim a few straggly hairs for appearance's sake. Never trim your dog's whiskers.

Dogs, with the exception of the curly-coated breeds, shed heavily twice a year—in the spring and fall. Shedding lasts about a month. This pattern varies tremendously, depending on the area of the country and the local weather conditions. The new coat will grow in three to four months. During the shedding season, brush your dog daily.

Nowadays, many of these practices are banned. Vets are not permitted to surgically alter a dog for show purposes. Banned procedures include modifying ear carriage by severing cartilage, straightening tail carriage by severing tendons, implanting plastic testicles in cryptorchids (dogs with no or only one testicle), and correcting the alignment of the teeth.

Some breeders have been known to try to manipulate ear carriage. While the dog is still a puppy, they will wax the insides of the ear flaps, use leather supports, or apply straps around the base of the ears. All of these procedures are illegal.

A dog's coat cannot be made uniform in color by plucking out stray hairs or by dying, tinting or bleaching. Chalk or talcum is permitted on white dogs, providing none remains in the coat during the show.

If a judge detects any illegal practices, he will disqualify the dog.

BATHING YOUR DOG

Most handlers recommend bathing a dog 24 hours before a show. Long-haired dogs are the exception to the rule, requiring more time between the bath and the show. The size of your dog dictates the best place to bathe him. A small dog fits nicely in the kitchen sink or a baby bathtub. Large dogs will need a large area–a wading pool or maybe just the garden hose in the backyard (providing the weather is warm), but many dogs end up in the bathtub.

Begin by placing the dog in the bathtub. Use a pitcher or hose to wet it down, starting at the back and working toward the head. Make sure the water is warm. Use a dog shampoo or a mild shampoo for people. Apply the shampoo in the same manner as you did the water, leaving the head for last. However, when you rinse the dog, begin at the head, working back. Squeeze out excess water and towel dry the dog. For puppies and toy dogs, you can use a hair dryer–but use it with caution, since the noise may frighten the dog. Unless your puppy has fleas or is really dirty, don't bathe him until he is six months old.

DENTAL CARE

Proper dental care is one of the most neglected aspects of pet care. Neglecting your dog's teeth can lead not only to diseases of the mouth and tooth loss but also to infections elsewhere in the body. Signs of dental disease include reluctance to eat, drooling, blood in the saliva, yellow-brown tartar at the gumline, broken teeth, and extremely bad breath.

As in humans, tartar accumulation causes periodontal (gum) disease. In the early stages of the disease, the gums become infected and inflamed. Plaque, a bacteria-laden film, forms on the teeth. The bacteria infects the gum tissue and then the roots of the teeth. The bones underlying the teeth begin to erode, the gums recede, and eventually the teeth fall out.

An amazing number of dogs suffer from periodontal disease–yet it is one of the most preventable diseases. You can help reduce tartar build-up by giving your dog dry food or dog biscuits. The best strategy, however, is brushing your dog's teeth. The idea of brushing your dog's teeth may sound ridiculous, but proper dental care is just as important for your dog as it is for you. When your dog is a puppy, massage his gums so he becomes accustomed to your hands in his mouth. To clean your dog's teeth, use a soft child's toothbrush or one that is designed especially for pets, and brush the teeth just as you would brush your own. Just a piece of gauze wrapped around your finger is helpful. Special toothpastes are also available, or you can use baking soda. Whatever you do, don't use toothpastes made for humans–they may make your dog gag. Besides, most dogs don't like the taste. Some vets recommend brushing your dog's teeth every other day; others suggest once a week.

Heavy accumulation of tartar may have to be removed under an anesthetic, which is costly for you and uncomfortable for your dog. So brush your dog's teeth and avoid this procedure if you can.

NAIL CARE

At some point, you will need to trim your dog's nails. The pavement helps to wear down the nails, but dogs that spend a lot of time indoors will need their nails trimmed fairly often. If you have never trimmed a dog's nails, it is a good idea to have a groomer or vet show you how. Guillotine-type clippers are good to use because they cut the nail, unlike plier-type clippers, which can crush the nail.

Be sure not to clip the quick of the nail (the blood vessel that runs through the nail). The quick has a nerve ending and, in addition to bleeding, will hurt your dog if cut. You can easily see the quick on dogs with white nails, but it narrows at the end so you will need to compensate for this. If you do draw blood, stop the bleeding with a styptic pencil. Be sure to check the dew claw (if present). These claws won't wear down on their own and can easily become ingrown if neglected.

The quick grows along with the nail. If you let the nail grow too long, you may end up cutting the quick to get the nail to a reasonable length.

As an alternative to clipping, some handlers recommend filing the nails back to the quick once a week.

EAR CARE

On a regular basis–every day or so if possible–examine your dog's ears. Like dental care, this is a good practice to establish when your dog is a puppy so that he will learn to stand still while you examine him. A show dog, in particular, must learn from an early age to readily accept handling.

Begin the exam by looking inside the dog's ear. The surface of the ear canal should be clean and have a similar appearance to the hairless part of the dog's belly. A little ear wax is normal, but if wax or hair is blocking the ear, it should be cleaned/plucked. (Warning: Don't attempt to clean your dog's ears unless your vet has shown you how.) If the ear has an unpleasant odor, consult your vet–this could be a sign of infection. When the daily ear exam is over, tell your dog what a wonderful and cooperative dog he has been.

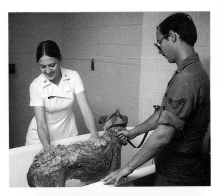

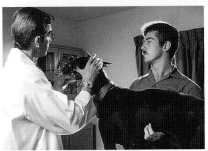

At top: Bathing a large dog may require teamwork–one person to wash the dog and another to hold him. *Above:* Dental care is an important but often neglected aspect of grooming.

Above: A plastic buoy called a bumper is used to teach a dog to retrieve a duck from the water. *Right:* The winner– Grand Hunting Retriever Champion David Chase with owner Dr Frank Schwartz.

OTHER COMPETITIVE EVENTS

A major focus of most kennel clubs is the conformation of a dog, but other types of competitive events are also held. The American Kennel Club conducts obedience trials, field trials, hunting tests and tracking tests. All of these events measure a dog's ability to perform a certain task. Every year more than 9000 events, including dog shows, are held under the authority of the AKC.

Obedience trials test a dog's ability to perform a prescribed set of exercises. Dogs compete on three different levels, with the ultimate goal of becoming an Obedience Trial Champion. These champions are granted the distinction of OT Ch before their names. Obedience trials are discussed in detail in the following chapter.

Field trials are practical demonstrations of a dog's ability to perform in the field the tasks for which the breed was developed. The titles awarded are Field Champion and Amateur Field Champion. These events are held for pointing breeds, retrievers and spaniels, as well as Beagles, Basset Hounds and Dachshunds.

Retrievers and pointing breeds may also compete in hunting tests, which evaluate a dog's hunting abilities. Winning dogs are awarded

Left: **Hunting Retriever competitions duplicate hunting conditions and situations. The dogs that participate in these events are extremely intelligent and well-trained.** *Above:* **Judge Connie Thibodeaux evaluates the performance of Jeff Devazier and his dog Widgeon.**

the title Junior Hunter, Senior Hunter or Master Hunter, after their names.

In a tracking test, a dog must follow a trail by scent. Dogs that pass this test earn a TD, or Tracking Dog, title. Passing a more advanced test entitles a dog to the letters TDX (Tracking Dog Excellent) after his name.

The United Kennel Club holds similar events. In keeping with this philosophy, six of the seven events conducted by the UKC are working events. Like those of other kennel clubs, the United Kennel Club Obedience Trials 'demonstrate the ability of the dog and its handler to work as a smooth functioning team.' Dogs registered with the UKC may compete for three titles: U-CD (United Companion Dog), U-CDX (United Companion Dog Excellent) and U-UD (United Utility Dog). While titles and classes are similar to those in the AKC, there are some distinct differences in the exercises themselves. The UKC has added an interesting feature to its basic heeling exercise. A dog must heel with a distraction in the ring–another dog in the ring. The second dog, called the Honoring dog, is in the down position. In the Novice and Utility classes the Honoring dog's handler is across the ring, while in the Open Class he is out of sight.

Within the UKC, there is the Hunting Retriever Club. 'Conceived by hunters for hunters,' the Hunting Retriever Club conducts licensed hunts designed to duplicate actual waterfowl and upland hunting conditions and situations. The participants dress in hunting camouflage and use decoys, duck calls, and duck blinds. Live and blank ammunition are also used.

Dogs compete individually against a recognized, established standard in three different skill levels–Started, Seasoned and Finished. The levels are based on the handler's skill and the dog's training, not on age. Dogs work toward the titles of Hunting Retriever, Hunting Retriever Champion and Grand Hunting Retriever Champion.

The UKC also offers a Hunting Beagle Program. This event is as close to a real hunt as possible. Dogs are cast free to hunt for wild

Above: **The Border Collie is adept at herding sheep and is a frequent winner at sheep dog trials. First begun in Wales in 1873 and in the United States in 1880, sheep dog trials are today held under the aegis of organized associations such as the International Sheep Dog Society in England, the North American Sheep Dog Society in Illinois and the American International Border Collie Registry in Iowa.**

rabbits with the goal of earning championship points. Taking of game is not allowed.

Reflecting its commitment to working dogs, the UKC holds competitions especially for Coonhounds: night hunts, field trails and water races. Each event is designed to test the hound's ability to perform under hunting conditions.

In the United States today, there are six major coonhound breeds: English Coonhound, American Black & Tan Coonhound, Bluetick Coonhound, Treeing Walker Coonhound, Redbone Coonhound, and the Plott Hound. The breeds can trace their origins back to the hounds brought over by the early settlers from England, Ireland, France and Germany.

SHEEP DOG TRIALS

For centuries sheep dogs have assisted man as he tended his flocks. While it is likely that many a shepherd has boasted about the skill of his herding dog, it wasn't until late in the nineteenth century that this skill was put to the test. The first known sheep dog trial was held in 1873 in Bala, North Wales. In 1906, a group of English and Scottish sheepmen formed the International Sheep Dog Society (ISDS).

Recognizing that a good sheep dog is priceless, the ISDS was dedicated to developing the ultimate sheep dog. To that end, the ISDS held sheep dog trials that reflected the true work of the shepherd. Trials today continue to demonstrate high standards of performance in handling stock, but to a certain extent have become a sport.

Sheep dog trials throughout the world are modeled after those held by the ISDS, with modifications based on differences in dogs, stock and conditions. In Great Britain, there are four national events leading up to the international trial. The top 15 dogs from England, Ireland, Scotland and Wales qualify for the international trial to compete for the Supreme Championship.

At the national championship trials, the handler stands at a post. Five sheep are released four hundred yards away. On the judge's order, the handler sends his dog, either to the left or to the right. The dog makes an 'outrun,' approaching the sheep from either a semi-circle or pear-shaped route. The outrun must be neither too close to the sheep nor too wide. When the dog gets to the opposite side of the sheep, he must pick up or 'lift' them, taking care not to upset them, and bring or 'fetch' them to the handler. The dog must guide the sheep between two obstacles and fetch them in as direct a line as possible.

For the next part of the exercise, called the drive, the dog takes the sheep around the handler, driving them 450 yards over a triangular course with two more obstacles, to the shedding ring. Two marked sheep are separated, or 'shed,' from the other three. On the judge's signal, the handler has the dog bring in the entire group of sheep to the pen. The handler may not assist the dog in any way. Once the sheep are penned, the handler closes the gate. The handler then releases the sheep and moves a single sheep to the shedding ring, where he must prevent it from joining the others. Sheep instinctively try to stay together, so this is no easy task.

The dog and handler have 15 minutes to complete the course. The scale of points is 20 points for the outrun, 10 for lifting, 20 for fetching, 30 for driving, 10 for shedding, 10 for penning, and 10 for the single sheep, for a total score of 110 points per judge. Four judges evaluate each dog and handler.

The international championship is the ultimate test of a herding dog's skill. Twenty sheep, in two groups, are released half a mile away from the dog, where the dog and often the handler cannot see them. The dog must gather one group of 10 and leave it and go back to gather a second group. After driving the twenty sheep through two sets of gates, the dog must shed five marked sheep and put them in a pen. The course must be completed in 30 minutes. For someone who has never seen a sheep dog in action these are truly fascinating competitions to watch.

In an effort to combat the hereditary eye diseases (PRA and Collie Eye Anomaly) that sheep dogs are prone to, the ISDS requires that all dogs entering the national and international competitions have their eyes examined by a veterinary ophthalmologist. Any dog who fails the eye exam is disqualified. Thus, breeders, who will naturally seek out the winning dogs, will be assured that the best sheep dogs are also healthy dogs.

Above: **A descendent of the sheep dogs that accompanied the invading Asian armies after the fall of the Roman Empire, the Briard remains an excellent sheep dog to this day.**

OBEDIENCE TRIALS

[Editor's Note: Unless otherwise specified, the rules that follow refer to obedience trials held under the authority of the American Kennel Club.]

In addition to bench shows, dogs can compete in obedience, field and working trials. At an obedience trial, dogs (all breeds can compete against each other) are judged on ability to perform a series of exercises, including heel on leash, heel free, retrieve on flat or over high jump and scent discrimination. Typically, German Shepherds, Golden Retrievers and Labrador Retrievers excel at this type of competition.

Obedience trials are much more than demonstrations of a dog's ability to follow specified routines in the ring. Rather, they illustrate the value of purebred dogs as companions. The AKC regulations stress that the purpose of obedience trials is to produce dogs that always 'behave at home, in public places, and in the presence of other dogs.' In the obedience ring, the dog and its handler are expected to perform accurately and correctly, but more importantly, the dog must show willingness and enjoyment.

Like bench shows, obedience trials are divided into classes: Novice, Open, and Utility. In addition to these regular classes, there are nonregular classes for such categories as veteran dogs and teams.

Above: A Bouvier des Flandres is moved around the ring at a conformation show. The trainer must move at a pace that is appropriate for the dog. Compare this trainer's pace to the pace of the woman on the *facing page*. Her dog, a West Highland White Terrier, is much smaller and therefore slower than the Bouvier, and she must adjust her pace to fit the dog's.

NOVICE CLASS

In the Novice Class, the exercises are Heel on Leash and Figure Eight (40 points); Stand for Examination (30 points); Heel Free (40 points); Recall (30 points); Long Sit (30 points); and Long Down (30 points). The maximum score is 200 points.

The Novice Class is for dogs over six months of age that have not won the title Companion Dog (CD). To win a CD certificate, a dog must have received qualifying scores in the Novice Class from three different judges at three obedience trials.

The **Heel on Leash and Figure Eight** exercise tests the ability of the dog and handler to work together. The handler enters the ring with the dog on a loose leash and stands with the dog sitting in the heel position. The handler may hold the leash in either hand or in both hands, as long as the hands are in a natural position. The judge will ask if the handler is ready and will then give the order 'Forward.' The handler gives the dog a command or signal to heel and the two of them move briskly but naturally. The dog must stay close to handler's left side and should not impede the handler's movement. Throughout the exercise the judge will give the orders for 'Forward,' 'Halt,' 'Right turn,' 'Left turn,' 'About turn,' 'Slow,' 'Normal' and 'Fast.'

The second half of the exercise requires the dog to Heel in a Figure Eight. At one point in the exercise, the judge will give the order 'Halt.' In this class, the Figure Eight is done on a leash.

If the handler is constantly tugging on the leash in an attempt to control the dog, or if the dog is unmanageable, the dog will receive a score of zero. Substantial points will be lost if the handler gives additional commands or signals to heel, or if the dog or handler fails to move at the proper speed following the orders for 'Fast' and 'Slow.' Deductions will also be made for lagging, heeling wide, crowding, poor sits, the handler failing to walk at a brisk pace, and occasional guidance with the leash.

In **Stand for Examination** the dog stands in position before and during the examination by the judge, showing neither shyness nor resentment. On the judge's order, the handler removes the leash from the dog and takes the dog to the spot indicated by the judge. The handler then positions his dog, gives it the command to stay, walks forward about six feet in front of the dog, turns around and stands facing the dog.

The judge will then approach the dog from the front and touch the dog's head, body and hindquarters. At the judge's order, 'Back to your dog,' the handler walks around behind the dog to the heel position. The dog must stay in position until the judge has said 'Exercise finished.'

Scoring typically begins when the handler gives the command to

Above: **The local dog show is a good way to learn the ropes.**

Above: **One way to teach a dog to stand is to bait him with food. Note the hand at the top of the photo. The unseen trainer is working with Oakdale's Sip of Scotch.**

stay. However, rough treatment by the handler or the dog's resistance to being put into position will be penalized severely. A dog that growls, snaps, displays shyness or resentment, or one that sits, lies down or moves away before or during the examination will receive a score of zero. Minor deductions will be made if the dog moves its feet at any time.

Heel Free is performed like Heel on Leash, except for the obvious difference of the dog being off the leash. A Figure Eight is not part of the exercise.

Recall tests a dog's ability to stay where left until called. On the judge's order, the handler gives the command or signal to stay in the sit position. The handler will then walk away from the dog about 35 feet across the ring, turn and face the dog, and, on the judge's order, give the command to come. The dog should immediately cross the ring at a brisk trot and sit right in front of the handler, close enough for the handler to reach out and touch the dog on the head. At the command 'Finish,' the dog must quickly move to the heel position and sit.

For the **Group Exercises**, the dogs–as a group–are required to remain in the sit or down position. For the **Long Sit** the handlers, on the judge's orders, command their dogs to sit and stay. The handlers then walk across the ring and face their dogs. If a dog gets up or is about to interfere with another dog, a steward will remove the dog from the ring. After one minute has elapsed, the judge gives the handlers the order to return to their dogs. Each handler must walk behind his dog to the heel position. The dogs must not move until the judge has said, 'Exercise finished.'

The **Long Down** is conducted in the same way as the Long Sit, except that the dogs are in a down position.

During these exercises, a dog must not move from the spot where he was left. Moving only a small distance will cause a deduction in points, while moving a substantial distance will result in a score of zero. A dog will also receive a zero if he does not remain in the proper position or if he barks or whines.

OPEN CLASS

The Open Class is divided into two sub-categories. The Open A Class is for dogs that have won the CD title but not the CDX, while the Open B Class is for dogs that have won the CD or the CDX title. The AKC issues the CDX (Companion Dog Excellent) certificate to dogs that 'have received qualifying scores in Open classes at three Licensed or Member Obedience Trials' from three different judges. A dog may continue to compete in the Open Class even after he has won the title UD (Utility Dog). The UD title is given to those dogs that have earned qualifying scores in the Utility Class at three different obedience trials from three different judges.

The exercises in the Open Class are Heel Free and Figure Eight (40 points); Drop on Recall (30 points); Retrieve on Flat (20 points); Retrieve over High Jump (30 points); Broad Jump (20 points); Long Sit (30 points); and Long Down (30 points). The maximum score is 200 points.

The **Heel Free and Figure Eight** exercise is performed in the same manner as the Heel on Leash and Figure Eight in the Novice Class, except that the dog is off the leash. The orders and scoring are identical to the Novice Heel on Leash and Figure Eight.

The **Drop on Recall** exercise builds on the Novice Recall. As with the Novice Recall, the handler, on the judge's order, gives the dog the command to stay and walks across the ring about 35 feet. On the judge's order, the handler commands the dog to come. As the dog is trotting briskly to the handler, the handler commands the dog to drop, and the dog must immediately drop to the down position, where he remains until the handler, on the judge's order, again gives the command to come. As with the Novice Recall, the dog must sit in front of the handler until commanded to sit at heel.

Drop on Recall is scored the same as the Novice Recall, with a few additional penalties. If the dog does not drop to the down position or does not remain down until called, he will receive a zero. Points will be deducted for delayed or slow responses to any of the commands.

Retrieve on the Flat tests a dog's ability to retrieve promptly. The exercise begins with the dog sitting in the heel position in a place designated by the judge. On the judge's order, the handler commands the dog to stay and throws a dumbbell at least 20 feet. If not thrown far enough or thrown too far to one side or too close to the ring, the judge will require that it be thrown again. When the judge gives the order 'Send your dog,' the handler commands the dog to retrieve. At a brisk trot, the dog should go directly to the dumbbell and immediately return to the trainer. The dog must sit right in front of the handler, close enough that the handler can take the dumbbell without having to move or stretch forward. On the judge's order, the handler will take the dumbbell from the dog. The exercise is finished in the same manner as the Novice Recall, with the dog sitting in the heel position.

The dumbbell, which must be approved by the judge, must be constructed of one or more pieces of heavy hardwood or of a rigid, nonwood material. Metal or hollow dumbbells are not allowed. The dumbbell can be unfinished, coated with a clear finish, or painted white, and its size must be proportionate to the dog.

A dog will receive a score of zero if he fails to retrieve on the first command, goes to retrieve before the command is given, does not return to the handler in the correct manner, or simply fails to retrieve. Points are lost for slowness in going out for or returning with the dumbbell, for not going directly to the dumbbell, for playing with the dumbbell, or for hesitating or refusing to give the dumbbell to the trainer. Points can also be lost for any of the applicable penalties explained under the Novice Recall.

Retrieve over High Jump adds the feature of jumping over a hurdle, or high jump, before and after the dog has picked up the dumbbell. During the exercise, the handler must stand at least eight feet from the jump, and he must throw it at least eight feet beyond the jump.

Above: **This Golden Retriever is being trained for the Long Sit. Soon the trainer will remove the leash during the lesson, and eventually dog and owner will head for the obedience ring.**

Above: **The first step in learning the Long Down. After putting the dog in the down position, the trainer tells her to stay and moves slightly away from the dog.**

The height of the jump is proportionate to the height of the dog. The jump is set at the nearest multiple of two inches to the height of the dog at the withers, or 36 inches, whichever is *less*, for the following breeds: Bloodhounds, Bernese Mountain Dogs, Bullmastiffs, Great Danes, Great Pyrenees, Greater Swiss Mountain Dogs, Mastiffs, Newfoundlands, and St Bernards.

The jump is set at the nearest multiple of two inches to the height of the dog at the withers, or eight inches, whichever is *greater*, for the following breeds: Clumber and Sussex spaniels, Basset Hounds, Dachshunds, Welsh Corgis, Australian Terriers, Cairn Terriers, Dandie Dinmont Terriers, Norfolk Terriers, Norwich Terriers, Scottish Terriers, Sealyham Terriers, Skye Terriers, West Highland White Terriers, Maltese, Pekingese, Bulldogs and French Bulldogs.

For all other breeds, the jump is set at approximately one and one-quarter the height of the dog at the withers. For example, the jump is set at 10 inches for dogs that measure from seven and one half inches to nine inches at the withers; at 12 inches for dogs that measure nine inches to less than 10.5 at the withers; at 14 inches for dogs that measure from 10.5 to less than 12 inches at the withers; and so on.

The judge will measure the dog on the field to ensure that jump is set at the proper height.

The exercise is scored like Retrieve on Flat. In addition, if a dog fails to go over the jump or climbs over the jump, he will receive a score of zero. Minor to substantial deductions will be made if a dog

hesitates before jumping or touches the jump as he goes over.

In the **Broad Jump**, the dog is required to leap over two to four hurdles, depending on his size. The distance covered by the broad jump is equal to twice the height of the high jump required for that particular dog. The hurdles are graduated in size, the last one being the highest, and each one is higher at the far end. Each hurdle is about eight inches wide, with the largest one about five feet wide and six inches tall at the highest point.

The exercise begins with the handler standing with the dog in a heel position about eight feet in front of the jump. The judge gives the order 'Leave your dog' to the handler, who commands the dog to stay and then walks to the right side of the jump. The handler faces the jump and stands with his toes about two feet from the jump, anywhere between the lowest edge of the first hurdle and the highest edge of the last hurdle.

On the judge's order the handler gives the command or signal to jump. The dog must clear the entire length of the jump and, without further command, return immediately to a sitting position in front of the handler, as in the Novice Recall.

A dog will receive a score of zero if he fails to stay until told to jump, refuses to jump on the first command, steps on or between the hurdles, or fails to clear the full distance. Points are lost if the dog does not return immediately to the handler, hesitates before jumping, or touches the jump.

The **Open Group Exercises** are performed like the Novice

Above: A Poodle leaps over a jump. The height of the jump varies with the size of the dog.

At top: **A woman begins teaching her Golden Retriever the scent discrimination exercise. The first step is to let the dog smell the object she is to retrieve.** *Above:* **The dog must then pick that item from a group of objects.**

Group Exercises, except that the handlers must leave the ring and be completely out of sight of the dogs. For the **Long Sit**, the judge will call the handlers back to the ring after three minutes; for the **Long Down** the handlers will leave the dogs for five minutes. The orders and scoring are the same as in the Novice Group Exercises.

UTILITY CLASS

The Utility Class is divided into two subcategories. The Utility A Class is for dogs that have won the CDX title but have not won the UD title, while the Utility B Class is for dogs that have won both titles.

The exercises for the Utility Class are Signal Exercise (40 points); Scent Discrimination Article No 1 (30 points); Scent Discrimination Article No 2 (30 points); Directed Retrieve (30 points); Moving Stand and Examination (30 points); Directed Jumping (40 points). The maximum score is 200 points.

The **Signal Exercise** demonstrates the ability of the dog and handler to work as a team while heeling and the dog's correct responses to the signals to stand, stay, drop, sit and come. The judge gives the same orders as in Heel on Leash and Figure Eight, with the addition of 'Stand your dog' and 'Leave your dog.' Using only signals, the judge will direct the handler to signal the dog to drop, to sit, to come—in that sequence—and to finish.

Throughout the Signal Exercise, heeling will be performed the same as in the Heel Free exercise, *except that the handler uses signals only and must not speak to his dog.* On the judge's order 'Forward,' the handler signals the dog to walk at heel. The judge then gives the orders 'Halt,' 'Right turn,' 'Left turn,' 'About turn,' 'Slow,' 'Normal' and 'Fast.' The orders may be given in any sequence.

While the dog is walking at heel, the handler, on the judge's orders, will give the signal to stand in the heel position and then the signal to stay. The handler will go to the other end of the ring and turn to face the dog. On separate and specific signals from the judge, the handler gives the signal to drop, to sit, to come, and to finish, as in the Novice Recall.

A dog receives a score of zero if he fails to obey a signal to stand, to remain standing where left, to drop, to sit and stay or to come the first time it is given. If the handler gives a verbal command rather than a signal for any element in this portion of the exercise, the score will be zero. Points will be lost if the dog walks forward on the stand, drop, or sit portions of the exercise, or if the handler gives a verbal command during the heeling or finish portions of the exercise.

The **Scent Discrimination** exercise tests a dog's ability to retrieve an article belonging to the handler based on scent alone. The handler gives the judge ten articles, from which he selects two articles to be set aside. The judge and the steward handle the other eight articles and place them on the floor or ground at random about six inches apart. The handler handles one of the articles that have been set aside and places it on the judge's book. Without touching the article, the judge places the article among the others. The handler and the dog will have their backs turned while the judge is placing the article on the ground. At this time, the handler may give his scent to the dog by gently touching the dog's nose with the palm of his hand.

On the judge's order to 'Send your dog,' the handler gives the command to heel and turns in place to face the articles. At the command to retrieve, the dog trots briskly to the articles. The dog is allowed to take a reasonable amount of time, providing he is working continuously. After picking up the article, the dog must quickly return to the handler and finish the exercise as in Retrieve on the Flat.

The same procedure is followed for the second article. If the dog retrieved the wrong article the first time, that article should be removed before the second attempt begins.

Deductions are the same as for Retrieve on the Flat and Novice Recall. A dog receives a score of zero if he fails to go out to the group of articles, retrieves a wrong article, or fails to bring the right article to the handler. Substantial deductions are made if the dogs picks up a wrong article, even though he puts it down immediately, if the handler is rough in giving the dog his scent, and if the handler fails to turn in place. Points are also lost if the dog is slow or inattentive, if he does not go directly to the article, or if he does not work continuously.

The **Directed Retrieve** demonstrates a dog's ability to retrieve an article that has been pointed out to him. While the handler and the dog have their backs turned, three white gloves are placed on the opposite side of the ring, one in each corner and one in the center. On the judge's order, the handler will give the command to heel and turn in place to face the gloves. The handler should not position his dog in any way. With his left hand the handler directs the dog to the glove specified by the judge, and with a verbal command, either simultaneously or immediately after the hand direction, sends the dog to retrieve the glove. At a brisk trot, the dog should go to the glove, pick it up without playing with it, and return to the handler, completing the exercise as in Retrieve on the Flat.

The handler is permitted to bend his body and knees, if necessary, when directing the dog to the proper glove, but otherwise must stand straight, in a natural position with his arms at his side.

Deductions are the same as for Retrieve on the Flat and Novice Recall. In addition, a dog receives a score of zero if he does not go directly to the glove, if he does not retrieve it, or if the handler gives a command or signal to position the dog to face the glove. A substantial deduction is made for not turning in place or not turning to face the glove. Minor to substantial deductions are made if the handler touches the dog or uses excessive motions while turning to face the glove, and for a handler who over-turns or touches the dog or uses excessive motions while turning to face the glove.

The **Moving Stand and Examination** tests the dog's ability to heel, stand and stay on command by the moving handler, accept the examination without shyness or resentment and on command return to the handler.

The handler stands with his dog sitting in the heel position at a

Above: **To complete the scent discrimination exercise, the dog brings the object back to the trainer, places it in front of her and sits at heel.**

Above: An owner gives her dog a pat on the head for successfully sitting at heel when they came to a halt during a practice session for the heel on leash segment of the Novice Class exercises. After a brief pause, the two of them begin (*facing page*) the figure eight.

point indicated by the judge. The judge asks, 'Are you ready?' and orders 'Forward.' The handler commands or signals his dog to heel and walks briskly at a normal pace. After the handler has proceeded about 10 feet, the judge orders 'Stand your dog.' The handler, without pausing, commands and/or signals the dog to stand, continues forward 10 to 12 feet and turns around, either to the right or left, to face the dog. The dog must stand and stay in position. The judge approaches the dog the from the front and examines the dog in a manner similar to a bench show examination.

When the judge gives the order 'Call your dog to heel,' the handler commands and/or signals the dog to return to the heel position. The dog must immediately return in a brisk manner to the proper heel position beside the handler.

A score of zero is given for the following: A dog displaying fear or resentment; moving from the place where he was left; sitting or lying down before being called; growling or snapping at any time during the exercise; repeated whining or barking; and the dog's failure to heel, stand and stay, accept the judge's examination, or return to the handler. Substantial to minor deductions are made for a dog that moves his feet repeatedly while in place, or for a dog that returns close enough to the handler but not to the heel position.

All appropriate penalties of the Novice Heel Free, Stand for Examination and Recall exercises apply. Minor or substantial penalties are made for the handler who changes the manner of walking or hesitates or pauses while giving the command and/or signal to stand, or if the dog fails to return briskly or sit properly in the heel position.

In the **Directed Jumping** exercise the dog demonstrates the ability to go in the direction indicated by the handler, stop when commanded, jump as directed and return as in the Recall. The exercise uses two jumps—a high jump and a bar jump. As in Retrieve Over the High Jump, the jumps are set based on the height of the dog.

On order from the judge, the handler commands and/or signals his dog to go forward at a brisk trot or gallop across the ring and then sit and stay. When the dog is sitting, the judge orders either 'High' or 'Bar' and the handler commands his dog over the designated jump. After the dog has taken the jump, he returns to the handler and finishes as in the Novice Recall.

When the dog is again sitting in the heel position, the judge asks, 'Are you ready?' before giving the order to send the dog over the other jump. The same procedure is followed for the second jump. Both jumps must be taken to complete the exercise and the judge must not designate the jump until the dog is at the far end of the ring. The dog must clear both jumps without touching them.

The height of the jumps is the same as required in the Open classes. The high jump is the same as used in the Open classes, while the bar jump consists of a bar between two and two and one half inches square with the four edges rounded to remove any sharpness. The bar is painted a flat black and white in alternate sections of about three inches each. It is supported by two unconnected four foot upright posts about five feet apart and is adjustable for each two inches of height, from eight inches to 36 inches.

A dog must receive a score of zero for the following: anticipating

Above: At the show—Champion Sundance's Southlake Legend and Oakdale's Sip of Scotch.

the handler's command and/or signal to go out, not leaving the handler, not going out between the jumps, not stopping on command and remaining at least 10 feet beyond the jumps, anticipating the handler's command and/or signal to jump, not jumping as directed, knocking the bar off the uprights, and climbing or using the top of the high jump for aid in going over.

Substantial deductions are made for a dog that does not stop in the proper spot in the ring; for a dog that turns, stops or sits before the handler's command to sit; and for a dog that fails to sit. Substantial or minor deductions are made for slowness in going out or for touching the jumps, or for any display of hesitation or reluctance to jump. All the penalties listed under Novice Recall also apply.

OBEDIENCE TRIAL CHAMPIONSHIP

Once a dog has earned the Utility Dog Title, he is eligible for championship points. Championship points are recorded for dogs that have earned a First or Second place ribbon competing in the Open B or Utility B, according to the schedule of points established by the Board of Directors of the American Kennel Club.

To become an Obedience Trial Champion, a dog must have won:
1. 100 points;

POINT SCHEDULE OPEN B CLASS

NUMBER COMPETING	POINTS FOR FIRST PLACE	POINTS FOR SECOND PLACE
6-10	2	0
11-15	4	1
16-20	6	2
21-25	10	3
26-30	14	4
31-35	18	5
36-40	22	7
41-45	26	9
46-50	30	11
51-56	34	13

2. a First place in Utility B, providing at least three other dogs competed;

3. a First place in Open B, providing at least six other dogs competed;

4. a third First place under the conditions of numbers two and three above; and

5. have won these three First places under three different judges, at all breed obedience trials, whether held separately or in conjunction with an all breed dog show.

Dogs that meet these requirements receive an Obedience Trial Championship certificate from the American Kennel Club. In addition, these dogs may use the letters O T Ch preceding their names.

NONREGULAR CLASSES

In addition to the classes discussed above, dogs can compete in various special–or nonregular–classes.

The **Graduate Novice Class** is for CD dogs that have not received their official certification for a CDX prior to the closing of

Above: A trainer works on the rudimentaries of down with her Golden Retriever. To be successful at an obedience trial a dog must willingly perform down, and be able to stay in that position for up to five minutes when the handler leaves the ring.

POINT SCHEDULE UTILITY CLASS

NUMBER COMPETING	POINTS FOR FIRST PLACE	POINTS FOR SECOND PLACE
3-4	2	0
5-7	4	1
8-10	6	2
11-13	10	3
14-16	14	4
17-19	17	5
20-23	20	7
24-26	24	9
27-29	27	11
30-32	30	13
33-36	33	14
37-40	37	15
41 and over	40	17

Above: **Two Golden Retrievers and their owner practice heeling in a brace and (*right*) sitting in a brace.**

entries. Dogs in this class may be handled by the owner or any other person. A person may handle more than one dog in this class, but each dog must have a separate handler for the Long Sit and the Long Down when judged in the same group. Dogs entered in the Graduate Novice may also be entered in one of the Open classes.

Performance and judging is the same as in the Regular classes, except that the Figure Eight is omitted from the Heel on Leash exercise. The exercises in the Graduate Novice class are Heel on Leash (30 points); Stand for Examination (30 points); Open Heel Free (40 points); Open Drop on Recall (40 points); Open Long Sit (30 points); and Open Long Down (30 points). The maximum total score is 200 points.

The **Brace Class** is for braces of dogs of the same breed that can do the Novice exercises. The dogs need not be owned by the same person, but must be handled by one handler. Dogs may be shown unattached or coupled, but whichever method is used must be continued throughout all exercises. A separate Official Entry Form must be completed in full for each dog entered.

Exercises, performances and judging is the same as in the Novice Class. Either or both dogs in a brace may be entered in another class or classes at the same trial.

The **Veterans Class** is for dogs that have an obedience title and are eight years years or older on the date of the trial. The exercises are judged and performed as in the Novice Class. Dogs entered in the Veterans Class may not be entered in any Regular class.

The **Versatility Class** is for dogs that are capable of performing the Utility exercises. Owners may enter more than one dog. Dogs in this class may be handled by the owner or any other person, and may be entered in another class or classes at the same trial.

Six exercises are performed, two each from the Novice, Open and Utility classes, except that there is no Group exercise. The exercises are performed and judged as in the Regular classes. For the purpose of this class, Scent Discrimination Articles Number One and Number Two are considered as a single Utility exercise. The exercises to be performed by each dog are determined by the handlers by drawing one of a set of cards listing combinations of the six exercise totaling 200 points. These cards are furnished by the trial-giving clubs. Each handler provides a dumbbell, Scent Discrimination articles and Directed Retrieve gloves. The exercises earn the following points: Novice exercise number one, 25 points; Novice exercise number two, 25 points; Open exercise number one, 35 points; Open exercise number two, 35 points; Utility exercise number one, 40 points; Utility exercise number two, 40 points. The maximum total score is 200 points.

The **Team Class** is for teams consisting of four dogs. An alternate dog may be entered, for which no entry fee is required. However, the same four dogs must perform all exercises. Dogs need not be owner-handled, need not be entered in another class at the same trial, and need not have obedience titles. A separate Official Entry Form must be completed in full for each dog entered.

There are two judges, one of whom calls commands while the other scores the teams' performances. The teams are judged one at a time, except for the Long Sit and Long Down exercise, which is done with no more than four teams (16 dogs) in the ring. The dogs on a team perform the exercises simultaneously and are judged as specified for the Novice Class, except that a Drop on Recall is used in place of the Recall exercise. In all the exercises except the Drop on Recall, the teams have the option of executing the judge's commands on the team captain's repeat of the command.

In the Drop on Recall exercise, the handlers leave their dogs simultaneously on command of the judge. The dogs are called or signaled in, one at a time, on a separate command from the judge to each handler. The handler, without any additional command from the judge, commands or signals his dog to drop at a spot midway between the line of dogs and the handlers. Each dog must remain in the down position until all four have been called and dropped. When the judge gives the command to call the dogs, they are called or signaled simultaneously. The finish is done in unison on command from the judge.

The scoring of the Team Class is based on the performance of the dogs and handlers individually, plus team precision and coordination. Each dog and handler is scored against the customary maximum, for a team total of 800 maximum available points. Individual dog's scores need not be recorded. The exercises and maximum scores are Heel on Leash, 160 points; Stand for Examination, 120 points; Heel Free, 160 points; Drop on Recall, 120 points; Long Sit, 120 points; and Long Down, 120 points. The maximum total score is 800 points.

Above: A brace of Golden Retrievers sitting at heel. To work together successfully in a brace, the dogs should already be trained to sit, heel and stay.

Above: **Judy Oehl and her English Springer Spaniel, Megan, practice a sit-stay.**

As you are training your dog to stay, watch closely for tell-tale signs that he is about to move—twitching his paw, restlessness—and correct him with a firm 'Stay!' *before* he moves. If he moves, put him back in place immediately.

GENERAL REGULATIONS FOR PERFORMANCE AND JUDGING

As in a bench show, the judge has a standard in mind. In an obedience trial, that standard is a mental picture of the perfect performance. In evaluating the dog, the judge looks for willingness, enjoyment and precision, while looking for naturalness, gentleness and smoothness from the handler. Speed is not a substitute for the dog's willingness to perform. Thus, lack of willingness or enjoyment on the part of the dog is penalized, as is lack of precision in the dog's performance, roughness in handling, military precision or peremptory commands by the handler. No penalties are less than one half point or multiple of one half point. A minor penalty is two and one half points or less; a substantial penalty is three points or more.

Each exercise begins with the judge asking 'Are you ready?' and concludes with 'Exercise finished.' Each dog is worked and judged separately except for the group exercises. When the judge has evaluated each dog, he will inform all handlers whether or not they qualified. To earn a qualifying score, the dog and handler must have received at least half of the available points in each exercise for a final score of at least 170 points.

All dogs must be kept on leash except when in the obedience ring or exercise ring. Dogs should be brought into the ring and taken out of the ring on leash. Dogs may be kept on leash in the ring when brought in to receive awards, and when waiting in the ring before and after the Group Exercises. The leash must be of fabric or leather and, in the Novice classes, should be long enough to provide adequate slack in the Heel on Leash exercise.

Dogs in the obedience ring must wear well-fitting plain buckle or slip collars. Slip collars can be leather, fabric or chain with two rings, one on each end. Fancy collars, or special training collars, or collars that are either too tight or so large that they hang down or not permitted. Nothing is allowed to hang from the collars.

Numerous times during an obedience trial, dogs are required to be in the heel position—whether the dog is sitting, standing, lying down, or moving at heel. According to AKC regulations, the heel position, is defined as the dog straight in line with the direction in which the handler is facing, at the handler's left side, and as close as practical to the handler's left leg without crowding, permitting the handler freedom of motion at all times. The area from the dog's head to shoulder should be in line with the handler's left hip.

AKC regulations also govern the handler's stance during the heel free. A handler has two options: 1. The handler's arms and hands must move naturally at the handler's sides while in motion, and must hang naturally at his sides while not in motion; or 2. The right hand and arm must move naturally, while the left hand is held against the body waist level.

In either case, the hands and arms may be adjusted during the Fast portion of an exercise, in order to maintain balance. Though these regulations may seem extreme to the newcomer, they must be adhered to or substantial deductions will be made. The reasoning behind this rule is that any movement on the part of the handler can be interpreted as a signal to the dog.

The handler's arms must be at his side during those exercises in which the dog is coming to him and sits in front. Again, a substantial deduction is made if a handler's arms and hands are not hanging naturally at his sides while the dog is coming in and until the dog has sat in front.

Whenever a command or signal is given, the handler may give a single command or signal only, and any extra commands or signals must be penalized. When AKC regulations specify 'command and/or signal,' the handler may give either one or the other or both command and signal simultaneously. When a signal is permitted and given, it must be a single gesture with one arm and hand only, and the arm must immediately be returned to a natural position. Signaling correction to a dog is forbidden and must be penalized. Signals must be inaudible and the handler must not touch the dog. Any unusual noise or motion may be considered to be a signal. Position of the arms and hands and movements of the body that aid the dog are considered additional signals. Whistling or the use of a whistle is prohibited. The dog's name may be used once immediately before any command.

Loud commands by handlers to their dogs have no place in an obedience trial. Shouting is not necessary even in a noisy place if the dog is properly trained to respond to a normal tone of voice. Commands which in the judge's opinion are excessively loud will be substantially penalized.

Praise and petting are allowed between and after exercises, but points must be deducted from the total score for a dog that is not under reasonable control while being praised. A handler may not carry or offer food in the ring or on the tracking field. A substantial penalty will be given for any dog that is picked up or carried at any time in the obedience ring.

Any display of fear or nervousness by the dog, or any uncontrolled behavior of the dog such as snapping, barking, or running away from the handler, whether it occurs during an exercise, between exercises, or before or after judging, must be penalized according to the seriousness of the misbehavior, and the judge may expel or excuse the dog from further competition in the class.

Handlers are not allowed to drill or train dogs while at an obedience trial, nor are dogs permitted to wear special training collars. Any handler who uses excessive verbal commands, moves toward the dog to correct him in any way, or practices any exercise in the ring will be excused from further competition in that class.

Above: It's important for dog and handler to maintain eye contact during a show.

THE MOST POPULAR DOGS IN THE WORLD

Above: **The Golden Retriever's friendly disposition has made the breed one of the most popular in the world. German Shepherd Dogs** *(facing page)*, **known as Alsatians in Great Britain, also enjoy worldwide popularity.**

What follows is an informal popularity contest based on the the number of breed registrations in the United States, England, Ireland, Australia and New Zealand. Medium large dogs from the hunting, working and herding classes are the most populous, with Labrador Retrievers, Golden Retrievers, German Shepherds and Rottweilers favorites in all of the aforementioned countries. Once man's invaluable assistant, these breeds have made a natural transition to trusted companion. Collies, Boxers and Dobermans are also prized. Of course, many people do not have the space to keep a good-sized dog, so it's not surprising that a number of the toy breeds make every country's list. Though many of the breeds turn up on every country's list, there are notable exceptions. Not surprisingly Australian Cattle Dogs are popular in their native country. Elsewhere, they are much rarer. Staffordshire Bull Terriers are popular in every country except the United States, where they rank only 101st.

THE TOP TEN

Compiling a definitive list of the world's top 10 most popular breeds based on numbers alone would be misleading, given that the United States simply has more dogs. For example, there are more Cocker Spaniels in the United States alone than there are Labrador Retrievers in the five countries surveyed. However, Labs are always listed in the top five, whereas Cocker Spaniels are popular only in the United States. The English Cocker Spaniel received an honorable mention because of its overwhelming popularity in all countries except the United States.

AMERICAN KENNEL CLUB REGISTRATIONS

Rank	Breed	Population
1	Cocker Spaniel	111,636
2	Labrador Retriever	91,107
3	Poodle	78,600
4	Golden Retriever	64,269
5	German Shepherd Dog	58,422
6	Rottweiler	51,291
7	Chow Chow	50,150
8	Dachshund	44,305
9	Beagle	43,314
10	Miniature Schnauzer	42,175
11	Shetland Sheepdog	39,665
12	Yorkshire Terrier	39,268
13	Shih Tzu	38,131
14	Pomeranian	32,109
15	Lhasa Apso	28,810
16	Chihuahua	24,917
17	Pekingese	22,986
18	Boxer	22,037
19	Siberian Husky	21,875
20	Doberman Pinscher	21,782

Rather than assigning a number ranking, we have listed the top 10 breeds in alphabetical order. The descriptions that follow are adapted from the American Kennel Club breed standards.

BOXER. In the nineteenth century German breeders crossed mastiff-type dogs with Bulldogs to create the perfect police dog—one that was ferocious and fearless but also able to jump walls and run at high speeds if pursuing a criminal. Though still used in Germany today as a police dog, Boxers are valued worldwide as pets.

Head: The broad, blunt muzzle is a distinctive feature of the breed and should be one third the length of the head. The skull is slightly arched with a deep stop. Wrinkles appear on the forehead when the ears are erect and are always present on the sides of the muzzle. The bite is undershot (the lower jaw extends beyond the upper) and curves slightly upward.

Eyes: The eyes are dark brown and, along with the wrinkling of the forehead, create the characteristic expressiveness.

Ears: The ears are set at the highest points on the sides of the skull. They are cropped long and stand erect.

Body: The chest is wide; the back short, straight and muscular. The neck is round, blending smoothly into the withers.

Legs and feet: The legs are long and well muscled. Feet are compact.

Tail: The tail is set high, docked and carried upward.

Coat: The coat is short, smooth and shiny.

Color: The colors are fawn and brindle. Fawn ranges from light tan to mahogany. Brindle ranges from sparse, clearly defined black stripes on a fawn background to a heavy black striping that nearly covers the background (reverse brindling).

White markings may cover up to one third of the total body color, but should not appear on the flanks or on the back of the torso. White on the face may replace the requisite black mask.

Gait: The gait is firm, yet elastic, the stride free and ground covering.

Character and temperament: The Boxer's bearing is alert, dignified and self-assured. With family and friends, the Boxer is playful, while with strangers he is wary but most importantly courageous if need be.

Size: Males are 22.5 to 25 inches at the withers; females are 21 to 23.5 inches.

COLLIE (ROUGH). The Collie is one of the most beautiful of all dogs. Originally bred as a herding dog in Scotland, the Collie today is primarily a show dog and a pet. Nevertheless, the breed retains the patience and intelligence for which it was initially developed.

Head: One of the most important features, the head is light, never massive. A heavy head detracts from the bright, alert expression. The head is shaped like a lean wedge with clean, smooth lines. It tapers gradually from the ears to the end of the black nose. The end of the muzzle is blunt, not square. Because the characteristics of the head are so important, faults are severely penalized.

Eyes: The eyes are almond-shaped, medium sized and set obliquely. Eye color is dark brown, except in blue merles, which may have one blue eye or partially blue eyes. The eyes of the Collie are clear, bright and inquisitive, especially when the ears are drawn up.

Ears: The ears are small, and when the dog is alert, they are carried erect, with the top one-fourth of the ear tipping or 'breaking' forward.

Neck: The neck is long, firm, clean and muscular, and is carried proudly, showing off the heavy frill.

Body: The body is long in proportion to height, with a deep chest. The back is strong and slightly arched over the loins. Hips and thighs are powerful.

Legs and feet: The legs are muscular. The hind legs are well bent at the stifles and are less fleshy than the forelegs. The comparatively small feet are roughly oval in shape. The soles are well padded and tough.

Tail: The tail is moderately long, with an upward twist on the end. It is carried low when the dog is quiet, and gaily but not over the back when excited.

Gait: The gait should suggest effortless speed and, in keeping with the dog's herding heritage, the ability to change direction almost instantaneously.

Coat: The coat is the Collie's crowning glory. It is long and abundant, especially on the mane and frill, but smooth on the face. The hair on the tail is profuse and on the hips it is long and bushy. The outer coat is straight and harsh to the touch, while the undercoat is soft, furry and so close together that it is difficult to see the skin when the hair is parted. (There is a Smooth variety of Collie that is identical in every way except for the coat, which is short, hard, dense and flat.)

Color: Collies are recognized in four colors: sable and white, tricolor, blue merle and white. Sable and white is predominantly sable, which ranges from shades of light gold to dark mahogany, with white markings on the chest, neck, legs, feet and the tip of the tail. A white blaze may appear on the foreface, skull or both. Tricolor is predominantly black with white markings placed like those of the sable and white, as well as tan markings about the head and legs. Blue merle is a mottled color, predominantly blue-grey and black with white markings like the sable and white and tan markings like the tricolor. White is predominantly white, with sable, tricolor or blue merle markings.

Size: Males are 24 to 26 inches at the shoulder and weigh from 60 to 75 pounds, while females are 22 to 24 inches and weigh from 50 to 65 pounds.

Expression: Expression is one of the most important characteristics of the Collie. The term is difficult to define because it cannot be described like color, height, weight and so on. In general, the Collie expression is best defined as 'the combined product of the shape and balance of the skull and muzzle, the placement, size, shape and color of the eye and the position, size and carriage of the ears. An expression that shows sullenness or which is suggestive of any other breed is entirely foreign.'

COCKER SPANIEL (AMERICAN). The smallest member of the AKC Sporting Group, the Cocker Spaniel has a sturdy, compact body and a cleanly chiseled, refined head. The Cocker is capable of consider-

At top: A Lhasa Apso puppy. As he matures, the top coat will grow heavy and long, a feature that provides protection from the harsh climate of Tibet, where the breed originated.

Above: A Boxer, with uncropped ears. In Great Britain, the practice of cropping a dog's ears is considered cruel and is prohibited. In the United States and many other countries, the practice is common and is, in fact, required for show dogs.

THE KENNEL CLUB OF ENGLAND

Rank	Breed	Population
1	German Shepherd Dog	14,650
2	Labrador Retriever	13,674
3	Golden Retriever	10,278
4	Yorkshire Terrier	9,368
5	Cavalier King Charles Spaniel	8,658
6	Rottweiler	7,598
7	English Cocker Spaniel	6,278
8	Staffordshire Bull Terrier	5,940
9	English Springer Spaniel	5,703
10	West Highland White Terrier	5,385
11	Doberman Pinscher	4,508
12	Boxer	4,480
13	Collie	3,579
14	Shetland Sheepdog	2,751
15	Bull Terrier	2,201
16	Great Dane	2,036
17	Cairn Terrier	2,006
18	Toy Poodle	1,958
19	Shih Tzu	1,755
20	Pekingese	1,607

able speed, as well as great endurance and shows enthusiasm for his work. Though the Cocker Spaniel is the number one breed in the United States, in other parts of the world, its cousin, the English Cocker Spaniel is far more popular.

Head: The well-proportioned head has a rounded skull with pronounced eyebrows and a definite stop. The muzzle is broad and deep, with square, even jaws. The teeth, which are strong and sound, meet in a scissors bite. The nose has the well-developed nostrils typical of a sporting dog. Black and black and tan dogs have a black nose, while dogs of other colors have a brown, liver or black nose. The eyeballs are round and full, although the shape of the eye rims suggests an almond shape. The appealing eyes of the Cocker express his intelligence and alertness. The long, well-feathered ears are set level or just below the lower part of the eye.

Neck and shoulders: The neck is muscular and long enough to allow the nose to reach the ground easily. Slightly arched, the neck tapers as it joins the head. The well-laid back shoulders and straight forelegs enable the Cocker to move with ease.

Body: With a deep chest and muscular hindquarters, the short, firmly knit body of the Cocker conveys a look of strength. The back slopes gently toward the tail. The Cocker Spaniel never appears long and low.

Tail: The docked tail is carried level with or just above the back. When the dog is in motion, the tail waves merrily.

Legs and feet: The legs are strongly boned and muscular. The forelegs are parallel and straight, while the hind legs show good angulation at the stifle and powerful, clearly defined thighs. The feet are compact, large, round, and firm, with horny pads.

Coat: On the head, the coat is short and fine, but on the body it is long enough to afford protection from rough ground cover. The feathering on the ears, chest and abdomen is full, but not so excessive that it hides the dog's true lines, nor hampers his function as a sporting dog. The texture of the coat is all important. It should be silky, flat or slightly wavy and easy to care for.

Color and Markings: The colors of the Cocker Spaniel are many and varied: black, including black with tan points; any solid color other than black (ASCOB) and any such color with tan points; or parti-color, which is two or more definite, well-broken colors, one of which is white. The tan points range in color from light cream to dark red and are located above each eye, on the sides of the muzzle and on the cheeks, on the undersides of the ears, on all feet and/or legs, under the tail, and on the chest. The markings should not compose more than 10 percent of the color.

Movement: Despite his small stature, the Cocker Spaniel moves with the gait of a sporting dog. His powerful hindquarters drive him forward, and the shoulders and forelegs give him considerable reach. Above all, the gait is coordinated, smooth and effortless.

Height: Males are 14.5 to 15.5 inches (15 inches is ideal), while females are 13.5 to 14.5 inches (14 inches is ideal).

COCKER SPANIEL (ENGLISH). According to the American Kennel Club registrations, the English Cocker Spaniel ranks 65th in popu-

larity. Outside of the United States, however, the English Cocker Spaniel is quite popular. Though similar in temperament to the American Cocker Spaniel, the English Cocker Spaniel is larger and not as heavily feathered.

Head: The head is a distinctive feature of the breed. The skull is arched and slightly flattened, with a distinct stop at the halfway mark. The muzzle is equal in length to the skull. The jaws are strong enough to carry game. The nostrils are wide, for scenting ability.

Eyes: The eyes are medium in size, full, slightly oval and set wide apart. The expression should be soft and melting, yet dignified, alert and intelligent. Eye color is dark brown, except in livers and particolors, which may have hazel eyes.

Ears: The ears are set low and close to the head, and are covered with long, silky hair.

Body: The neck is graceful and muscular, blending into the shoulders in a smooth curve. The compact, well-knit body conveys a look of strength without heaviness. The chest is deep; the back short, sloping gradually towards the tail.

Tail: Ideally, the docked tail is carried level and is in constant motion while the dog is in action.

Legs and feet: The legs are fairly well boned and muscular. The feet are firm, round and catlike, with arched toes.

Coat: The coat is of medium length, with a silky texture. The hair can be either flat or slightly wavy. On the head, the coat is fine and short.

DACHSHUND. Once a badger hunter in Germany, the low slung Dachshund is prized today for his lively and courageous personality. The Dachshund carries himself with a bold and confident carriage.

At top: **The English Cocker Spaniel, a friendly dog with an affectionate and cheerful temperament.** *Above, right:* **A Dachshund and the Longhaired variety** *(above)*. **Once used to hunt badgers, today Dachshunds are primarily kept as pets.**

THE AUSTRALIAN NATIONAL KENNEL COUNCIL

Rank	Breed	Population
1	German Shepherd Dog	8989
2	Rottweiler	7095
3	Australian Cattle Dog	3700
4	Labrador Retriever	3390
5	Chihuahua	3169
6	Golden Retriever	2910
7	Doberman Pinscher	2725
8	Boxer	2665
9	English Cocker Spaniel	2620
10	Bull Terrier	2618
11	Border Collie	2678
12	Staffordshire Bull Terrier	2561
13	Poodle	2425
14	Maltese	1994
15	Australian Silky Terrier	1870
16	Cavalier King Charles Spaniel	1853
17	Collie	1830
18	Dachshund	1771
19	Welsh Corgi Pembroke	1533
20	Shetland Sheepdog	1249

Head: The head tapers uniformly to the tip of the head. The skull is slightly arched, sloping gradually, without a stop to the muzzle. The bones over the eyes are prominent, and the jaws are powerful. The neck is fairly long and muscular.

Eyes: The eyes are medium in size, oval and set at the sides of the head. The color ranges from a dark reddish brown to brownish black.

Ears: The ears are set high and back on the head. They are long and well rounded.

Body: The Dachshund is long and muscular. The back is straight, arching slightly at the loins. The chest is strong, with a prominent breastbone.

Tail: The tail forms a continuation of the spine. The standard specifies that the tail 'should not be carried too gaily.'

Legs and feet: The legs are muscular and extremely short in relation to the long body. The forelegs turn inward slightly. The paws are compact, with arched toes.

Coat: There are three varieties of Dachshunds: Shorthaired (Smooth), Wirehaired and Longhaired. Except for the difference in coat, they are identical in conformation. The coat of the Shorthaired is short, thick, smooth and shining. The Wirehaired has a tight, short, thick, rough, hard coat, with a soft undercoat, similar to the coat of the German Wirehaired Pointer. A Wirehaired Dachshund has a beard and bush eyebrows. The Longhaired Dachshund has long, silky hair, with feathering on the legs, underside and tail. The elegant coat is reminiscent of that of an Irish Setter.

Color: Accepted colors for all varieties are red, red-yellow, yellow and brindle, with or without a shading of interspersed black hairs. Two-colored Dachshunds can be deep black, grey or white, with tan markings, the most common being black-and-tan. Dappled Dachshunds are a clear brown, grey or white ground color, with dark, irregular patches of dark-grey, brown, red-yellow or black. Neither the light nor the dark color should predominate.

Size: The Dachshund varies considerably in size, ranging from 16 to 30 pounds. There is also a miniature version that weighs under 10 pounds.

DOBERMAN PINSCHER. This excellent guard dog owes its agility and toughness to one man's dedication to creating the perfect breed. That man was Louis Dobermann.

Head: The long head resembles a blunt wedge. The top of the skull is flat, with a slight stop. The cheeks are flat and muscular, the jaws full and powerful.

Eyes: The eyes are almond shaped and moderately deep set. Eye color is medium to dark brown.

Ears: The ears are usually cropped and carried erect.

Body: The Doberman is a medium-sized dog, with a square body. The back is short, firm and muscular. The chest is broad, with a well defined forechest and well sprung ribs. The stomach is well tucked up. The hips are broad, roughly the same width as the shoulders. The well arched, muscular neck is carried proudly.

Legs and feet: The legs are long, sinewy, well muscled and heavily boned. The feet are well arched, compact and catlike.

Gait: The gait is free, balanced and vigorous.

Coat: The coat is smooth, short, hard, thick and lies close to the skin.

Color and markings: The accepted colors are black, red, blue and fawn (Isabella). The rust markings are sharply defined, appearing above each eye and on the muzzle, throat and forechest, on all legs and feet, and below the tail. The nose is solid black on black dogs, dark brown on red dogs, dark grey on blue dogs and dark tan on fawn dogs.

Size: Male dogs are 26 to 28 inches, ideally about 27.5 inches, while females are 24 to 26 inches, ideally about 25.5 inches.

GERMAN SHEPHERD DOG. Known as the Alsatian in Great Britain, the German Shepherd Dog impresses one with his strength and agility. The breed became popular in the United States and Great Britain following World War I, when soldiers returning home brought the dogs with them.

A well balanced and well muscled animal, the Shepherd is alert and full of life. The dog is longer than he is tall, with smooth curves rather than angles. The ideal dog has the mark of quality and nobility–a look that is hard to define but immediately recognizable.

Character: The German Shepherd Dog has a distinct personality, evidenced by his direct and fearless–never hostile–expression. He is self-confident but somewhat aloof, although he is approachable and willing to meet overtures. The German Shepherd Dog is poised, and when occasion demands, eager and alert, as demonstrated by his success as a companion, watchdog, guide dog, herding dog or guardian.

In the show ring, a dog must never be timid or nervous. The judge must be able to examine the teeth of the dog, and any dog that attempts to bite a judge will be disqualified. The ideal dog has the body and gait of a working dog, along with an incorruptible character.

Head: The strong and cleanly chiseled head of the German Shepherd Dog is best described as noble. The head of the male is distinctly masculine, while that of the female is distinctly feminine. The skull slopes into the long, wedge-shaped muzzle without abrupt stop. The moderately pointed ears open toward the front and are carried erect. The eyes are medium sized, almond shaped, and as dark as possible. The expression is keen and intelligent.

Neck: The neck is strong, muscular and long. When the dog is excited or alert, the head is raised and the neck carried high.

Feet: The feet are short and compact, with toes well arched, pads thick and firm, and nails short and dark.

Body: The build of the dog suggests depth and firmness. The chest is deep, with well-sprung ribs. The abdomen is firmly held and only moderately tucked up. The withers are high and slope into the straight and very strong back.

Tail: The tail is bushy, hanging in a slight curve like a saber when at rest. When the dog is excited the curve is accentuated and the tail raised.

Above: German Shepherds are highly intelligent and capable of performing a wide range of responsibilities, from police work to guiding the blind.

THE IRISH KENNEL CLUB

Rank	Breed	Population
1	Labrador Retriever	909
2	English Springer Spaniel	860
3	German Shepherd Dog	856
4	Shih Tzu	848
5	West Highland White Terrier	549
6	English Cocker Spaniel	504
7	Rottweiler	459
8	Collie	457
9	Golden Retriever	345
10	Poodle	286
11	Boxer	268
12	Irish Setter	261
13	Cairn Terrier	250
14	Old English Sheepdog	233
15	Dachshund	199
16	Welsh Corgi Pembroke	198
17	Kerry Blue Terrier	197
18	English Setter	195
19	Staffordshire Bull Terrier	190
20	Doberman Pinscher	174

Gait: The gait is smooth-flowing, elastic and seemingly effortless, covering the maximum amount of ground with a minimum of steps. The hindquarters deliver, through the back, a powerful forward thrust that slightly lifts the whole animal and drives the body forward.

Coat: Of medium length, the dense double coat lies close to the body. The hair is straight and harsh, and shorter on the head and inner ears.

Color: Most colors are permissible, although the darker colors are preferred. White dogs can be registered with the American Kennel Club, but will be disqualified from competition in the show ring.

Height: Males are 24 to 26 inches, while females are 22 to 24 inches. The German Shepherd Dog is longer than he is tall, with a 10 to 8.5 length to height ratio the preferred proportion.

GOLDEN RETRIEVER. The Golden Retriever is a symmetrical, powerful, active dog, sound and well put together, not clumsy nor long in the leg. His expression is amiable, and his personality eager, alert and self-confident. Primarily a hunting dog, he should be shown in hard working condition. In the ring, overall appearance, balance, gait and purpose is given more emphasis than any of the component parts. The Golden's friendly, mellow personality and beautiful, golden coat have made this breed one of the best-loved dogs in the world.

Head: The skull is broad, with a well-defined but not abrupt stop. The muzzle appears straight in profile, blending smoothly and strongly into the skull.

Eyes: The eyes convey a friendly and intelligent expression. They are medium large and set well apart, preferably dark brown in color. Dogs with functional abnormalities of the eyelids or eyelashes (such as trichiasis or entropion) should be excused from the ring.

Teeth: The teeth meet in a scissors bite. Misalignment of teeth or a level bite is a fault, while an undershot or overshot jaw disqualifies.

Nose: The nose is black or brownish black, though fading to a lighter shade in cold weather is not a serious fault. A pink nose or one lacking in pigmentation is a fault.

Ears: The ears are set high on the head and are not too long. When pulled forward, the tips of the ears should just cover the eyes.

Neck: The neck is medium long, merging gradually into well laid back shoulders, giving a sturdy, muscular appearance. The Golden has an untrimmed, natural ruff.

Body: The Golden Retriever is an athletic dog, with a muscular build. The body is neither long nor overly compact. The chest is wide and well-developed, but not barrel chested.

Feet: The Golden's feet are medium-sized, round and compact, with thick pads. Excess hair may be trimmed to show natural size and contour.

Tail: The tail is thick and muscular at the base. It is carried with merry action, level or with some moderate upward curve, never curled over the back nor between the legs.

Coat: As befits a hunting dog, the Golden's coat is dense and water repellent with good undercoat. The outer coat is firm and resilient,

neither coarse nor silky, and may be straight or wavy. There is moderate feathering on the back of the forelegs and on the underbody; heavier feathering is found on the front of the neck, the back of the thighs and underside of the tail. The coat on the head, paws and front of legs is short and even. The feet may be trimmed and stray hairs neatened, but the natural appearance of the coat or the outline should not be altered by cutting or clipping.

Color: A Golden Retriever should be a rich, lustrous golden of various shades, providing it is not extremely pale or dark. Feathering may be lighter than the rest of coat, but any white marking, other than a few white hairs on the chest, should be penalized. Allowable white shadings are not to be confused with white markings. Latitude is given to a light puppy whose coloring shows promise of deepening with maturity.

Gait: When trotting, the Golden has a smooth, powerful and well coordinated gait, showing good reach. As speed increases, feet tend

Above: **Few things can match the charm of a litter of playful Golden Retriever puppies.**

NEW ZEALAND KENNEL CLUB REGISTRATIONS

Rank	Breed	Population
1	Rottweiler	1838
2	German Shepherd Dog	1493
3	Labrador Retriever	1061
4	Golden Retriever	536
5	Welsh Corgi Pembroke	476
6	Boxer	470
7	Doberman Pinscher	413
8	Cavalier King Charles Spaniel	403
9	Staffordshire Bull Terrier	403
10	Dachshund	373
11	Bull Terrier	354
12	Chihuahua	281
13	Poodle	263
14	English Cocker Spaniel	261
15	German Shorthaired Pointer	237
16	Border Collie	236
17	Weimaraner	227
18	Rhodesian Ridgeback	227
19	Collie	225
20	Beagle	207

to converge toward the center line of balance. Dogs should be shown on a loose lead to reflect the true gait.

Size: Males are 23 to 24 inches in height at the withers, while females are 21.5 to 22.5 inches. Dogs up to one inch above or below the standard size will be penalized; dogs that deviate more than an inch from the standard will be disqualified. Also important is the height-to-length ratio. The length from the breastbone to the point of the buttocks is slightly greater than the height at the withers in a ratio of 12:11. An adult male should weigh between 65 and 75 pounds, while females should weigh between 55 and 65 pounds.

Temperament: Goldens are well known for their friendly, reliable and trustworthy personalities. Quarrelsomeness, hostility, timidity or nervousness are not in keeping with the Golden's character and should be penalized.

LABRADOR RETRIEVER. The Labrador Retriever wins the award for the most popular dog in the world. Labs make wonderful family pets: they are good tempered, amiable and loyal. Excellent with children, the easy-going Lab will not fail to defend his charges if the need arises.

The general appearance of the Labrador is that of a strongly built, short-coupled, very active dog. The ideal Lab should be fairly wide over the loins, and strong and muscular in the hindquarters.

Head: The skull should be wide, with a slight stop; the jaws long and powerful. The nose is wide, with well-developed nostrils. Teeth should be strong and regular, with a level mouth. The ears hang moderately close to the head, and are set rather far back and somewhat low. The eyes should be of a medium size, expressing great intelligence and good temper, and can be brown, yellow or black, but brown or black is preferred.

Tail: A distinctive feature of the breed, the medium-length tail is thick near the base, gradually tapering towards the tip. Free from feathering but covered with the Labrador's short, thick, dense coat,

the tail has a rounded appearance, which has been described as an 'otter' tail. The tail may be carried gaily but should not curl over the back.

Coat: Another distinctive feature, the coat should be close, short, dense and free from feathering, and should have a fairly hard feel to the hand.

Color: Black, yellow, or chocolate. Yellows may vary in color from fox-red to light cream, with variations in the shading of the coat on the ears, the underparts of the dog, or beneath the tail. A small white spot on the chest of any color Labrador is permissible.

Height: Males are 22.5 to 24.5 inches, females 21.5 inches to 23.5 inches.

Weight: Males are 60 to 75 pounds, females 55 to 70 pounds.

POODLE. The Poodle is active, intelligent and elegant. He is squarely built, well proportioned and carries himself proudly. When clipped in the traditional fashion, the Poodle has an air of distinction and dignity peculiar to himself.

Head and expression: The skull is moderately rounded, with a slight but definite stop. The muzzle is long, straight and fine. The strong teeth meet in a scissors bite. The dark eyes are oval in shape and alert in expression. The ears hang close to the head and are set at or slightly below eye level. The ear leather is long, wide and thickly feathered.

Neck and shoulders: Rising from strong, muscled shoulders, the neck is strong and long enough to carry the head high and with dignity.

Body: The chest is deep and moderately wide, with well sprung ribs. The back is level, and the loins short, broad and muscular.

Tail: The docked tail is straight, set on high and carried up.

Coat: The coat is curly, harsh and dense. The hair grows indefinitely and is not shed, so it must be clipped. A Poodle under a year old may be shown in the Puppy clip. Dogs one year or older must be shown in the English Saddle or Continental clip. In Nonregular classes, Poodles may also be shown in the Sporting clip.

In the Puppy clip, the face, throat, feet and base of the tail are shaved. The entire shaven foot is visible, and there is a pompon on the end of the tail. The coat may be shaped so that it has a neat appearance and a smooth line to it.

In the English Saddle clip, the face, throat, forelegs and base of the tail are shaved, leaving puffs on the forelegs and a pompon on the end of the tail. The hindquarters are covered with a short blanket of hair except for a curved, shaved area on each flank and two shaved bands on each hind leg. The rest of the coat may be shaped to give it overall balance.

The Continental clip requires that the face, feet, throat and base of the tail be shaved. The hindquarters are shaved, leaving optional pompons on the hips. The legs are also shaved, with bracelets on the hind legs and puffs on the forelegs. As with the English clip, the entire shaven foot and a portion of the shaven foreleg above the puff are visible. Again, the coat may be trimmed to give it balance.

In the Sporting clip, the face, feet, throat, and base of the tail are

Facing page: **With their gregarious personalities, Labrador Retrievers have captured the hearts of dog lovers all over the world.** *Above:* **The Golden Retriever's heritage as a hunting dog is reflected in the breed's dense, water repellent coat. A rich golden color, the coat is feathered on the front of the neck, along the back of the forelegs and on the underbody. The back of the thighs and the underside of the tail are also feathered.**

Originally bred as hunting dogs, Poodles were also renowned as circus performers in France. Today, however, they are best known as family pets. The Standard variety existed first, and from it the Toy *(above)* and Miniature *(right)* varieties were developed.

shaved, leaving a cap on the top if the head and a pompon on the end of the tail. The coat on the body and legs is covered with a short blanket of hair, about an inch in length, trimmed to follow the outline of the dog. The hair on the legs may be slightly longer on the legs than on the body.

In all clips, the hair on the top of the head may be gathered in an elastic band.

Color: The coat is solid and evenly colored and may be blue, grey, silver, brown, cafe-au-lait, apricot, cream, white or black. Brown and cafe-au-lait Poodles have liver-colored noses, eye rims and lips, dark toenails and dark amber eyes. Poodles of the other colors have black noses, eye rims and lips, black or self-colored toenails and very dark eyes.

Gait: The Poodle moves with a light, springy step, carrying his head and tail up.

Size: The Standard Poodle is over 15 inches at the withers; the Miniature Poodle is over 10 and less than 15 inches; and the Toy Poodle is less than 10 inches.

ROTTWEILER. The forbears of this muscular dog are believed to have crossed the Alps from Italy to southern Germany with Roman soldiers. By the Middle Ages the local people used the dogs to drive cattle to market, a task that was supplanted by the railroads in the nineteenth century, nearly forcing the breed into extinction. Today, however, the Rottweiler is popular throughout the world.

Head: The head is of medium length and broad between the ears, with well developed cheekbones and stop. The muzzle is straight and broad, tapering slightly at the tip. The nose is broad rather than

This page: **Rottweilers are extremely intelligent dogs, with a strong desire to work. In spite of their stocky appearance, they are agile dogs.**

round. The lips are always black. The Rottweiler has 42 teeth, meeting in a scissors bite. Four or more missing teeth or an undershot or overshot jaw will disqualify a dog from the ring.

Eyes: The almond shaped eyes are medium sized and moderately deep set. Eye color is medium to dark brown, the darker the better.

Ears: The pendant ears are triangular in shape and small in proportion to the head. They are set well apart, making the head seem even broader.

Neck: The neck is powerful, well muscled and moderately long.

Body: The Rottweiler is deep chested, with a firm and level back. The compact build suggests great strength, agility and endurance.

Tail: The short tail continues the straight lines of the back. The tail is docked at birth, although some dogs are born without a tail or with a very short stub.

Legs and feet: The legs are long, powerful and heavily muscled. The feet are round and compact, with well arched toes. The back feet are somewhat longer than the front.

Coat: The outer coat is straight, coarse and dense. The hair is of medium length and lies flat against the body.

Color: The Rottweiler is always black with well defined markings. Markings are rust to mahogany in color and are placed as a spot above each eye; a strip on the sides of the muzzle; on the throat; a triangle on either side of the breast bone; and on each leg, slightly below midleg, down to the toes. Quantity and location of markings is important and should not exceed 10 percent of body color.

Gait: The Rottweiler is a trotter and has a sure, powerful step.

Character: The dog has a fearless expression and an inherent desire to protect home and family. Rottweilers are intelligent, hard-working animals. They have a tendency to be self-assured and aloof.

Size: Males stand 24 to 27 inches, females 22 to 25 inches. Males are heavily boned and more masculine in appearance.

INDEX

Photo Credits

AGS Archives 51 (left)
Animals Unlimited 6, 9 (all), 11 (right), 18, 23, 24, 36, 46 (left), 48 (left), 62, 63, 83 (all), 85 (top and bottom right), 92 (all)
Sherry Baker Krueger 47 (left), 67, 78, 91
Marie Cahill 29 (left), 32, 55 (left)
Kathy Castillo 56, 57 (top left)
Dalmatian Station via RE DeJauregui 12
RE DeJauregui 1, 28 (left), 39, 40, 43, 44, 45, 47 (right), 53, 54 (all), 55 (left), 64, 65, 74, 75, 79
Jeff Devazier 60 (left), 61 (all)
DOD Msgt Ken Hammond 17, 87
Dogs For the Deaf 34 (bottom), 35
Dr. Amanda Fennig, DVM 4 (top center), 8, 10 (bottom), 13 (all), 16, 20, 21, 23, 25 (all), 26, 27, 28 (right), 29 (right), 30, 38, 42, 43 (left), 57 (left), 68, 70, 71, 72, 73, 75, 76 (all), 77, 91
Jayne Langdon 11 (left), 37, 40 (right), 41
Oakdale Labradors, Joyce and Jim Woods, Montevallo, Alabama 4 (bottom), 10 (top), 40 (left), 46 (right), 55 (right), 57 (right), 60 (right), 66, 80, 90, 91
Robert and Eunice Pearcy 2-3, 7, 14, 15, 19, 22 (right), 31, 33, 34 (top), 48 (right), 49, 52, 69, 81, 85 (left), 89, 96
Anthony Sanders 93 (right)
USAF 59 (all)
USAFE MSgt Pat Nugent 51 (right)

Overleaf: **The Bouvier des Flandres has a naturally rugged appearance. In the past, the Bouvier served as an ambulance and messenger dog, while today he acts as a family friend and guardian.**